Seven Hours to Sundown

SEVEN HOURS TO SUNDOWN

a play by
GEORGE RYGA

Vancouver, Talonbooks, 1977

copyright © 1977 George Ryga

published with assistance from the Canada Council

Talonbooks
201 1019 East Cordova
Vancouver
British Columbia V6A 1M8
Canada

This book was typeset by Linda Gilbert of B.C. Monthly Typesetting Service, designed by David Robinson and printed by Hemlock Printers for Talonbooks.

First printing: December 1977

Talonplays are edited by Peter Hay.

Rights to produce *Seven Hours to Sundown*, in whole or in part, in any medium by any group, amateur or professional, are retained by the author and interested persons are requested to apply to him at Ryga & Associates, P.O. Box 430, Summerland, B.C. V0H 1Z0.

Canadian Cataloguing in Publication Data

Ryga, George, 1932–
    Seven hours to sundown

      ISBN 0-88922-124-3 pa.

      I. Title.
    PS8585.Y4S4   C812'.5'4   C78-002056-1
    PR9199.3.R9S4

Seven Hours to Sundown was commissioned by Theatre Network and The University of Alberta and first performed at the Studio Theatre at The University of Alberta on May 27, 1976, with the following cast:

Sid Kiosk	Dennis Robinson
Tom Rossini	Jonathan C. Barker
Irma Kiosk	Tanya Ryga
Janice Webber	Shay Garner
Jerry Goyda	Juergen Beerwald
Del Kiosk	Jonathan C. Barker
Jeff Dolan	Jonathan C. Barker
The Man	Jonathan C. Barker

Directed by Mark Manson
Designed by Victor Becker
Assistant Designer and Lighting by Gerry Zelinski

LIST OF CHARACTERS

SID KIOSK, *the mayor*
TOM ROSSINI, *an alderman*
IRMA KIOSK, *a young woman*
JANICE WEBBER, *a newspaper woman*
JERRY GOYDA, *an ex-schoolteacher and craftsman*
DEL KIOSK, *the father of the mayor*
JEFF DOLAN, *the newspaper publisher*
A MAN.

SET

A non-set stage.

Scene and location changes are accomplished by movement of coastered hardware. Two chairs, a desk and a telephone bring the mayor's office onstage. A workbench for leather tooling brings the environment of JERRY GOYDA on the set. A metal typing desk, through physical activity around it, becomes the offices of the newspaper.

Entry positions of these various elements of the set, once established, are maintained, such as: stage right for the mayor's office; stage left for GOYDA's workshop; centre backstage for the newspaper office. Scenes which are imagined or which come out of the past are played centrestage forward in an area isolated with light.

Act One

The lights come up slowly.

Drum and harmonica music are heard, played in a driving rhythm.

JANICE WEBBER enters, singing, bringing on her part of the set.

JANICE: *singing*
    In our town
    The grass grows green
    The air is fresh
    The water's clean
    No one's poor
    An' no one's mean
    At seven hours to sundown . . .
    In our town
    Seven hours to sundown . . .

    There is a drum and harmonica interlude before the next stanza.

JANICE:
> In our town
> There is much to do
> The bus an' transports
> Drive right through
> We all grow beans
> An' lilacs, too
> At seven hours to sundown . . .
> In our town
> Seven hours to sundown . . .

>> *The music continues for another interlude. JANICE picks up and opens a back issue of the newspaper that she writes for. The music ceases. She reads aloud from the paper.*

Last week's civic elections in Woodlands were no surprise to this newspaper or to seasoned political observers in this community. A low-keyed, lack-lustre campaign ended in a low-keyed, lack-lustre election of members to town council. Less than thirty percent of eligible voters cast ballots, in an election which saw the victory of Sid Kiosk as mayor, winning by a margin of eight votes over his opponent, hardware merchant John Henderson.

>> *KIOSK enters with his portion of the set. He is studying the newspaper as well. He is annoyed with what he reads in the paper and, using the telephone on his desk, dials a number.*

KIOSK:
> Hullo, Dolan? Sid Kiosk here. . . . I'm not happy about your damned editorial . . . not one bit! . . . How come Henderson gets identified as a hardware merchant an' I just get named? . . . I've advertised farm produce with you. I don't like it when bigger advertisers get free plugs for their businesses out of an election campaign. An' I don't like that insinuation that deadbeats got elected this time. . . .

Running the town is a big job these days. . . . I ran a good, vigorous campaign. . . . Yeah? Well, you tell her then!

> *KIOSK hangs up the telephone and reads on in the paper.*
>
> *In the following dialogue, DOLAN might speak through an intercom.*

DOLAN: *offstage*
Janice!

JANICE:
Yes, Mister Dolan?

DOLAN:
Ease up on that goddamned new mayor, will you?

JANICE: *smiling*
Yes, Mister Dolan.

DOLAN:
Maybe you could run a two-column photo of him cutting some ribbon . . . or petting a carrot . . . or kissing a kid. Something to make him happy.

JANICE:
Yes, Mister Dolan.

DOLAN:
You're a good kid, Janice. Learn and listen . . . and in twenty years, who knows? You might leave home, go twenty miles down the road, and work for the Highlands Herald!

> *He laughs.*

Even Randolph Hearst started small!

JANICE laughs, then reads on in her copy of the paper.

JANICE: *reading*
>The election also saw the return of Tom Rossini as alderman. It is hoped that this alderman, who has shown strong initiative in the past as a developer, might demonstrate an equal vitality in the public office to which he was elected, a quality noticeably absent in his previous term in office.

ROSSINI enters KIOSK's area of the stage and offers a handshake to KIOSK. He then settles back comfortably in a chair.

ROSSINI: *warmly*
>Congratulations, Sid . . . I voted for you, in case it matters.

KIOSK:
>If everyone who's come forward since the election to say they supported me *had* voted for me as they claim, I'd have come in on a landslide.

He points to the paper in front of him.

>See what they've written about you?

ROSSINI:
>Yes.

KIOSK:
>Sue them!

ROSSINI:
>What for? . . . I got in, didn't I? . . . Any publicity is better than none. People remember reading about a man. They soon forget whether it was good or bad.

DOLAN: *offstage*
>Janice!

JANICE:
>Yes, Mister Dolan?

DOLAN:
>Keep a low profile on that bastard, Rossini, will you? . . . He doesn't need any help taking over the town.

JANICE:
>He's not exactly a ball of fire, Mister Dolan. At most council meetings he doesn't even bother voting.

DOLAN:
>He doesn't have to. He fixes things so the voting goes the way he wants, whether he's there or not. Look at his investment record sometime . . . I've got it here in my office. His assets doubled during his first term as alderman.

JANICE: *surprised*
>I didn't know that.

ROSSINI: *speaking to KIOSK*
>Nobody knows much about the inner workings of civic government . . . an' they care less. So . . . I came to congragulate you, and to offer any help I can give, in . . . showing you the ropes, as they say.

KIOSK: *coldly*
>Appreciate that, Tom. But the outgoing mayor has given me as much help as I'll need.

ROSSINI:
>Well, in case . . . I offered.

KIOSK:
>No need, but thanks all the same, Tom.

>>*JERRY GOYDA enters with his portion of the set. He is followed by IRMA KIOSK. She is agitated.*

IRMA:
> Let's give Rossini his notice. . . . The church will cost sixty dollars a month, and we'll have three times the studio space to work in!

GOYDA:
> Hold on, Irma . . . nothing is quite as simple as it appears at first.

IRMA:
> I've checked it out . . . look!

>> *She takes out some scraps of paper from her handbag and spreads them in front of GOYDA.*

ROSSINI: *speaking to KIOSK*
> So . . . you made it as mayor.

KIOSK:
> Would appear so.

>> *He tries to make himself busy with his paperwork.*

ROSSINI:
> I never had any desire for that. . . . Too much like being a foreman of a work crew. You get all the responsibility. If anything goes wrong, it's you who gets the blame.

KIOSK: *irritated*
> Somebody has to.

ROSSINI:
> It's been a long time since we worked together . . . or had any dealings.

KIOSK:
> You've done alright without me.

ROSSINI:
>Your family, are they well? ... Your daughter, Irma, was it? ... Where's she now?

KIOSK: *struggling to be civil*
>My wife had an operation on her shoulder, but she's fine now. Irma went to Winnipeg, but came back last summer...

>*He becomes thoughtful.*

IRMA: *speaking to GOYDA*
>Heat, light and water ... a total cost of nine hundred a year ... including a trade licence if we were to set up a retail store in the lobby.

>*GOYDA examines the papers more closely.*

ROSSINI:
>Is she living at home, then?

KIOSK: *sharply*
>Yes, she's livin' with us!

ROSSINI:
>I'm sorry if I said something...

KIOSK:
>Dammit, you had no kids! ... She's a good person ... helps out with work, pays her room an' board. ... A bright, beautiful girl ... but ...

GOYDA: *speaking to IRMA*
>Where did you get these figures?

IRMA:
>At the municipal office.

GOYDA:
>It doesn't mean anything. That old church has been vacant for five yers.

IRMA:
> I took the volume of services used in the past, multiplied it by two, then calculated charges on the current cost of services . . . added a trade licence . . . two hundred dollars for maintenance an' repairs and . . .

> *GOYDA throws up his arms.*

GOYDA:
> Okay, Irma . . . right, love . . . I've got it! What shape's the church in?

> *IRMA closes her eyes and recites the facts.*

IRMA:
> It's seventy-two years old . . . frame construction . . . stucco exterior and three-quarter inch plaster interior . . . hot water system installed in the parish hall next door . . . good roof . . . some windows cracked . . . seven rooms . . . pine floors . . .

KIOSK:
> She's got no ambition . . . doesn't go out. Lots of nice young men have phoned or come around to the house . . . but Irma looks right through them. Spends all her time . . . even Sundays . . . in that grubby little leather shop on Elm Street.

ROSSINI:
> The place run by Jerry Goyda?

KIOSK:
> Yes . . . Goyda.

ROSSINI:
> Ah, but maybe Goyda is . . .

> *He leers at him.*

KIOSK:
>I don't want to hear what you gotta say about that . . . not a word! I brought my child up good. . . . That's not a man. . . . I told him that myself once when I was on the school board an' saw to it he wasn't teaching in our schools no more. To cut leather and sew buttons is not a man's way of making a living, an' nothing's ever going to change my way of thinking!

>*Both men stare at each other.*

GOYDA: *speaking to IRMA*
>Who owns it now?

IRMA:
>When the parish dissolved itself, the church reverted to the municipality for back taxes.

GOYDA:
>But wasn't there a service club . . . or some lodge leasing parts of the complex?

IRMA:
>The Masons lease the parish hall one night a month. It can all be cleared up at the municipal offices . . . my dad's mayor now . . . and Alderman Rossini is the contact for the lodge holding partial lease.

GOYDA:
>Don't jump to any conclusions where those two are concerned.

IRMA:
>They're good men . . . everybody does what they have to do. Sometimes we don't understand. . . . I don't like to see us gouged for rent by Rossini, but other than that . . .

GOYDA:
> Stop being a child, Irma. I've been up and down that whole route . . . from the Teachers' Federation to part-time helper in a village mortuary.

IRMA:
> And what did you learn from it all?

GOYDA: *considering his reply*
> That it takes a lot of effort to stay out of fights. That the serenity of a small town is nothing more than a slower-witted killer stalking his prey!

> > *During the last speech, JANICE has pushed her newspaper aside, stretched languidly and, gathering her handbag and notebook, gone to where KIOSK and ROSSINI are.*

JANICE:
> Have you gentlemen any statement to make for the next issue of the paper?

KIOSK: *foolishly*
> Why should we?

IRMA: *addressing GOYDA*
> That's an awfully suspicious attitude to have.

GOYDA:
> Never mind my attitudes . . . hold this. I need to cut a yard of lacing.

> > *IRMA holds the leather for him while he cuts.*

JANICE:
> You're the politicians. I merely report on your deliberations.

ROSSINI:
> Nice girl, eh, Sid?

KIOSK:
> I don't know about that. I don't like what she writes. But I don't suppose many people read the paper, except for the ads an' help wanteds.

> *He grins at his own witticism. ROSSINI is watching JANICE closely.*

JANICE:
> I was passing by . . . saw two heads through the window. Thought maybe some startling new civic development was under consideration by the two crackerjacks on town council.

ROSSINI:
> Like hell you were, Janice. We're both old enough to be your father. . . . I wish you'd remember that.

JANICE:
> Then I've come as an enemy of the people . . . looking for information to ridicule the choices of the electorate . . . thirty percent of the electorate, but who wants to know?

ROSSINI: *speaking to KIOSK*
> Mouth like a garage door, but a nice girl! Like Mussolini. . . . When my grandfather was fading, he began to admire Mussolini . . . for the same reasons I admire her!

KIOSK:
> I don't know anything about that. . . .

> *He addresses JANICE.*

> What can I do for you, young lady? I'm busy getting into harness, as you can appreciate. But you can count on my co-operation . . . if for no other reason, than to keep information you write a bit more truthful!

JANICE: *smiling sweetly*
    That's nice!

KIOSK:
    Think nothing of it. Now . . . I have work to do.

    JANICE rises and, nodding to ROSSINI, leaves. She moves back to her office.

    KIOSK and ROSSINI go into a soundless discussion.

IRMA: *speaking to GOYDA*
    I think *you* should write the letter of application for a lease. Coming from me . . . well . . . my old man's the captain now, and it would look a bit . . .

GOYDA:
    Embarrassing?

IRMA:
    It's a small, conservative town. The idea of converting the oldest remaining church into a workshop or business premises . . . I *like* him . . . the idea may not rest easy with people who supported him. You know . . .

GOYDA:
    Be decisive, for God's sake. You came in with everything, including a business licence . . . now what?

IRMA: *confused*
    You don't understand. I was born and raised here. You're an outsider.

GOYDA:
    I've lived here fifteen years . . . my teaching career began and ended here . . . thanks to your father. I've developed a business here . . . most of my friends are here.

IRMA:
> You're still an outsider.

GOYDA:
> What makes an insider? The ability to see every point of view three different ways?

IRMA:
> No. It's the inability to see one point of view, Jerry!

GOYDA:
> So it's screw Rossini and his rent rip-off one minute, and be nice doing it the next. I enjoy doing what I do, but sometimes I would like a break. You came in with an idea, and I say, "Fine! Let's move on it." But I don't like having it left in my lap. Your father and I have a grudge going back many years. . . . You've got a share in this shop. It would be easier for you to approach him.

IRMA:
> Alright, I will. But you write the letter.

GOYDA:
> Why?

IRMA: *floundering*
> Because . . . you're in charge . . . here.

> *GOYDA nods. The lights go out on the scene. GOYDA exits.*

> *When the lights come up, IRMA is seated in front of KIOSK. The setting around them has lost the officious appearance of the mayor's office. The setting could be the mayor's home, or might indicate a closeness between two people who are in reality separated by a failure of communication.*

KIOSK:
> No!

IRMA:
> No, what, Dad?

KIOSK:
> I said no, and I'll say it again.

IRMA:
> The proposal is reasonable . . . the church has been empty a long time now.

KIOSK:
> He could come in person to ask me. Why does he write a letter as if I lived in another country? When I told him I didn't approve his lack of discipline in the classroom . . . that his contract would not be renewed . . . I called him into the school board office and told him face to face. Goyda, I said, we need children who can learn to do things, not just vote. They vote or not once every three or four years . . . but every morning, they'll be getting up to go to work.

IRMA:
> I still hear people say he was a good teacher.

KIOSK:
> Then let him teach somewhere else. I didn't stop him teaching. I only stopped him teaching *here*! He had no right getting his hooks into you . . . opening up a useless shop . . . looking poorer an' poorer. He did it to bother me . . . everything he's done was for that reason.

IRMA:
> He didn't get any hooks into me. I would rather do crafts than work at a nine-to-five job.

KIOSK:
> If you'd said that, I could've opened a shop for you.

IRMA:
> I don't want a shop. . . . I only want to do what I like doing.

KIOSK: *thoughtfully*
> Is there anything . . . between you and him?

IRMA:
> Do I like him?

KIOSK:
> There's not much of a man there . . . a knitter . . . a shoelace tier!

> *He is angry now.*

> Whatever you call it! . . . You're with him half the night sometimes!

IRMA:
> Yes . . . I like him.

KIOSK:
> What about *him*, eh?

IRMA:
> He's not like that. . . . He works very hard . . . reads . . . takes long walks by himself . . . listens to music on Sundays.

KIOSK:
> He doesn't work hard. He amuses himself . . . like a professional card player, or piano tuner. I don't understand why a child of mine can't see through all that nonsense.

IRMA:
>He works hard . . . long hours. He reminds me of my grandfather, Dad.

KIOSK:
>The old man would turn over his his grave if he heard you say that, Irma! There was a man for you . . . took on the world with two hands. Always said the Kiosks would become people to look up to . . .

>>*DEL KIOSK, IRMA's GRANDFATHER, enters, an old, beaten man out of the past.*

>Tell them, Pop! Tell 'em how it used to be!

>>*The GRANDFATHER peers uncertainly into the gloom. He throws back his shoulders irritably.*

GRANDFATHER:
>The carrots . . . one helluva poor job you done hoeing them carrots, boy!

KIOSK: *disturbed*
>Tell 'em how you told Williston to get his goddamned truck off the yard when he delivered a load of twisted lumber for the new greenhouse! You told that deaf old bastard off good, I remember that!

GRANDFATHER:
>'An the Deering girl . . . you were the one got her in trouble. . . . Joe Deerin's come to see me about it.

KIOSK: *plaintively*
>I don't love her, Pop!

GRANDFATHER:
>Damn the lovin' . . . you're gonna do what's right by her. If she leaves you, that's another thing. But you're gonna do the right thing an' marry her!

> *KIOSK is shaken. IRMA rises to her feet. She is a small girl, frightened.*

IRMA:
    Dad?

KIOSK:
    He was tough as nails, runnin' that carrot farm single-handed . . . morning to night. I helped him when I could . . . after work . . . on weekends.

GRANDFATHER:
    All alone . . . in sickness or in health . . . all alone I worked them fields, growin' carrots for shoe salesmen, the blacksmith an' his family . . . Slippery Jess, the lady with the boardinghouse . . . Slippery Jess, they called 'er!

> *KIOSK grasps at what small details he can to sustain himself.*

KIOSK:
    But you never let anyone have a free ride on a Kiosk, Pop! You sure told that Williston off when he tried that trick with bad lumber . . .

GRANDFATHER:
    Five o'clock in the morning, frost on the ground, my back achin' so I could hardly stoop . . . but there I was, haulin' sacks of carrots to the railway station. Had to be in when they was still cold. . . . People who don't grow their own food don't buy anythin' which don't taste or feel like it just come out of the ground. Five o'clock in the mornin', and I'm out there workin'. The Chinaman in town, he don't work half as hard . . . sits in his store all day an' sells chewin' gum an' French safes to boys like my son.

KIOSK:
    I told you and I meant it, Pop, that one day a Kiosk would be on top in this town!

GRANDFATHER: *leaving*
>Five o'clock in the morning, an' I'm hauling sacks of cold carrots like I'm some coolie movin' a rock pile. My son's asleep . . . his overheated wife's asleep . . . they're all sleepin' still.

>*The GRANDFATHER exits.*

IRMA:
>Dad . . . I'm sorry about Grandfather. And Mom leaving. . . . I feel like I'm to blame for a whole lot of things that went wrong.

KIOSK: *wiping the tears from his eyes*
>It's nothing. We've still got our health. An' people respect your old man, Irma. With the newspaper against us, we showed them! Your old dad is mayor of this town . . . from a carrot farm to mayor . . . and if I do well, I'll run again and do it twice!

IRMA:
>We . . . didn't do it. I never supported your campaign, Dad.

KIOSK: *momentarily hurt*
>Others did, so what the hell? Wish the old man had lived long enough to see it happen. . . . In his lifetime, you know, we were treated like low-level scruff in this town.

IRMA:
>Don't talk about it if it hurts you. It's not important to me.

KIOSK:
>But it's important to me, young lady!

>*He is growing annoyed and restless.*

>I wanted to be an engineer, but I couldn't get away from that goddamned farm. Then there was the

business with your mother . . . and her going to live with that bone-headed rancher, Stark. You know what he does when he should be repairing fences in the spring?

IRMA:
No, I don't.

KIOSK:
He flies kites! She told me once he's even won awards for it. . . . Like a kid, he flies goddamn kites!

IRMA:
But . . . what difference does it make now, Dad?

KIOSK:
What difference? Somebody has to care if our world's to survive from one day to the next. Do you think life goes on as if by accident? No damned way. . . . There are people everywhere making sure roofs don't leak . . . that machinery is oiled an' ready to go . . . that food reaches the tables . . . that roads get repaired an' cleared. I resent people like your friend, Goyda, who hangs on to the system with one hand an' thumbs his nose at the stars with the other! He's not the first. . . . There were others before him in this town!

IRMA:
I don't know what you're talking about.

KIOSK:
Remittance men. . . . Lazy, insolent Englishmen who came to this country with a monthly retainer of money to keep them here. My old man came over as a working immigrant. *They* came like royalty . . . bought up the best farming land an' left it in bush. My old man wants to farm, but he gets the gravel to farm on. They bring their relatives over on holidays . . . drive up to our farm an' show us off as if we were their hired labour! They never learned

to say my old man's name, even though he emigrated from the same country they did.... "Hey, chappie," they'd call to him, an' wag their forefingers as if they were calling a dog.... "Hey, chappie, come over and mow my lawn tomorrow." ... an' he did. Goddamn him, but he did!

IRMA leaves while KIOSK is deeply preoccupied with his thoughts. Slowly, he mobilizes himself and begins to sort through the papers on the desk in front of him.

ROSSINI enters and paces about in front of KIOSK's desk.

ROSSINI:
Still working, Sid?

KIOSK:
Yes.

ROSSINI:
Come on to the Legion. I'll buy you a beer.

KIOSK:
I don't drink beer. It makes me drowsy.

ROSSINI:
You doing work, or making work?

KIOSK:
What the hell does that mean? I spend a lot of time in here.... I was elected to spend time here. Sometimes I'm in this office until midnight ... thinkin'.

ROSSINI:
Thinking what?

KIOSK:
>Thinking for the rest of you.... You guys come into council meetings Monday nights.... Bert Jones is pissed.... Some of you sleep here.... I seen Will McIntyre dozing last week ... an' voting away eight thousand for road repairs. He votes, but he doesn't know what for. The bastard comes to council meetings to sleep, so he can be in shape for his night job at the trailer plant after he leaves the meeting!

ROSSINI:
>You worry for all of us, is that it?

KIOSK:
>You damned right I do!

ROSSINI:
>I'm glad I'm not mayor.

KIOSK:
>I wish you'd all start to shape up.... Water mains breaking like they were made of glass. Dinners to attend, speeches to make ... for what? To keep the town from falling apart, that's for what!

ROSSINI:
>Stop campaigning ... you're elected now.

KIOSK:
>Then don't provoke me.

ROSSINI:
>Your daughter came to see me at my office today. She wants my support for her partner's application to lease the old church.

KIOSK: *annoyed*
>Why did she do that?

ROSSINI:
> I don't want to lose the rent they pay on the shop they're in. But . . . I don't want that thrown in my face if it comes to a vote in council.

KIOSK:
> So you promised you'd support Goyda . . . after I'd already told her I'm opposed?

ROSSINI: *grinning*
> The art of politics, my friend, is the art of kissing a homely woman . . . as you push her out the door into the street. Your daughter spoke to me. I listened sympathetically, nodded and promised her nothing.

KIOSK:
> Yeh . . . I see.

> *He is thoughtful.*

> You figure my daughter's homely?

ROSSINI: *coughing into his fist*
> No. I was only explaining how I deal with life.

KIOSK:
> Get this straight, Rossini . . . I don't want Goyda getting into that church. I know it's personal . . . if I wasn't mayor . . . if I hadn't had dealings with him in the past, I'd be the first to support his application. But that's not the case. . . . I don't like the guy or what he does an' thinks. So if he gets in, it's over my objections . . . and my loss of face. That's the way I read it, an' I'm too old to change. That sonofabitch stays where he's at!

ROSSINI:
> That's fair enough with me. He's a good tenant. And it may complicate the lease our lodge has with the community. But we have to come up with something reasonable for council to make its decision on.

KIOSK:
>   What do you mean?

ROSSINI:
>   You can't face the other aldermen and say that sonofabitch stays where he's at . . . I don't like him personally, and Rossini, his landlord, doesn't want to lose rent!

KIOSK:
>   I'm new to the job. Can't you come up with something?

ROSSINI:
>   My suggestion is to wear him down by asking for further information . . . more presentations. Give him encouragment, but not a committment. In the end, we can always hang him on a technicality.

>   *KIOSK is confused by this expanation.*

KIOSK:
>   I'm a farmer, not a manipulator in real estate.

ROSSINI:
>   Don't start weighing in what you do for a living against what I do. . . . You want a problem resolved, I'm offering a suggestion, that's all.

KIOSK:
>   I don't like telling lies to people. It's either yes or a no. . . . What you're saying bothers me. I remember your old man tried to punch out my old man for a piece of his farm. . . . That's in the past, but I don't forget. I'd prefer some way of refusing Goyda's application.

ROSSINI:
>There is no way. Any short cuts through the system means somebody ends up with a bloodied nose. In this case, it'd be your nose. I won't support you. Neither would the riff-raff passing for aldermen in this town.

KIOSK:
>I see what you mean. . . . Okay . . . we got to think.

>*They huddle into a wordless conversation.*

>*GOYDA and JANICE enter into GOYDA's stage area. GOYDA brings with him a parcel and drops it on the floor at the back of his table.*

GOYDA:
>The smaller the supply order, the higher the mailing charges. Also, my discount percentage drops. A business can't stay small anymore. You *pay* to maintain a shop this size.

JANICE:
>You're undercapitalized . . . marry a rich widow.

GOYDA:
>I don't want a crafts supermarket. Is there no other option?

JANICE:
>Not for a man. They're on the downslide. The day is coming when men will be hiring out to houseclean and mend clothes for working women. Of course, they'll be eligible for alimony support from wives who divorce them, so the picture is not altogether desperate.

>*GOYDA laughs.*

GOYDA:
> You're a joy to see first thing in the morning, you know that? Cheerful, wise, consoling . . . a mother hen to a worried man. . . . Get out of my shop!

JANICE: *laughing*
> Has Irma been by yesterday?

GOYDA:
> She's on a mission. I've got seven handbags to bead and three leather vests to lace, but everything slows to a crawl when Irma's on a mission.

JANICE: *holding up a handbag*
> I'd like this one . . . when it's finished.

GOYDA:
> Not until you've paid for the last one you took.

JANICE:
> But I've explained . . . I left it on a seat at the movie when I went to get a drink. When I returned, it was gone. . . . I haven't got it.

GOYDA:
> I'm in the business of selling handbags, not theft insurance. You owe me fourteen ninety-five!

> *JANICE laughs.*

JANICE:
> That's the retail price, for Christ's sake, Jerry.

GOYDA:
> You're not a wholesaler. Buy twenty and I'll give you a discount by jobbing. Otherwise, you owe me fourteen ninety-five.

JANICE:
> You're serious, aren't you?

GOYDA:
>Yes, I am. There are too many things in this shop getting carted away by my friends.

>>*The lights go out on KIOSK and ROSSINI.*

JANICE: *whining*
>When I've paid my rent from what I earn at the newspaper, there's almost nothing left.

GOYDA:
>So what am I supposed to do? Subsidize your income with hand-tooled leather handbags? ... Go away, I'm busy.

JANICE: *holding the handbag lovingly*
>It's beautiful ...

GOYDA:
>Alright, I'll make you a proposition, Janice. If we get space in the old church, I'll expand business. You can then put in some part-time work here. I'll talk to Irma about what we can afford to pay.

JANICE:
>You're putting me off. Irma doesn't know business from her asshole. ... What's the latest on the church?

GOYDA:
>Kiosk is cold. I knew he'd be. Irma's working on the others.

JANICE:
>You're too small to take on such a large building, Jerry.

GOYDA:
>Well, I'm suffocating in this place. It's cluttered . . . it's a pressure-tank of contradictions. I work with leather and bone all day . . . but each time I look up I get an accusing eyeful of Greenpeace Save the Whales posters. Blubber's bad this season, but every ecologist I know is working leather. When I mention this paradox, I get a dead stare.

> *JANICE gives him a long, dead stare. GOYDA grins.*

JANICE:
> Under that long hair . . . under the skin . . . you're really a law and order type.

GOYDA: *still grinning*
> That's right . . . and I believe in justice, and in an honest day's wages for an honest day's work!

JANICE: *caustically*
> And in marriage . . . and retirement fund contributions!

GOYDA:
> As a matter of fact, that, too. . . . When I was at university, I lived with a woman . . . for three years we stayed together. She had my child . . . a son. Stephen, we called him.

> *JANICE is startled. GOYDA turns away from her. A MAN in a bizarre costume enters and stops a short distance from GOYDA. He avoids looking at GOYDA, his face shaded by a large dark hat.*

MAN:
> She's not comin' back. . . . She told me to go see you and tell you that she's not comin' back.

GOYDA:
>Marlene met some charlatans with yet another religious vision of how to save the world. She took Stephen with her. . . . When the prophet finally came to lean on my door-frame to tell me, she had been gone three months.

MAN:
>I'll tell you so you'll know, the brothers and sisters will kick your ass if you try comin' around makin' trouble. . . . She's happy with us.

GOYDA:
>Filthy scruff dressed in rags . . . elementary school drop-outs too weak and stupid to make it in petty crime. . . . Tuned in to Christianity with jackboots!

MAN:
>You got to speak to me sometime, man. . . . You can't just stand there lookin' at me like that. . . . I don't like anyone lookin' at me that way!

GOYDA: *turning away from him*
>Ignorance has an odour . . . a sauerkraut barrel stench. It was beginning to fill my room, my eyes, my life . . . with him standing there only a few minutes.

MAN:
>The kid's been christened Ezekiel . . . that's his name now. She's been christened, too. Her name's Diana. If you ever see them, you're gonna call 'em that, you understand?

GOYDA:
>Ignorance not only stinks. It inflicts pain.

MAN: *gloating*
Your kid's my kid now! He's never goin' to any school. I'm gonna teach him everythin' . . . how to be a high priest. When he grows up, he's gonna punish her. . . . I'm gonna teach him how. . . . He's gonna punish her an' any sister who smokes, drinks, eats meat or fornicates!

GOYDA:
Ignorance inflicts pain by breaking your ribs when your back's turned . . . bruising your liver . . . breaking a tooth with the toe of a boot . . .

>*Almost as if it were in slow motion, the MAN attacks GOYDA from behind. He knocks him to the ground, then kicks at his ribs, face and back with his booted feet. GOYDA makes no effort to protect himself. He rolls and twists with the blows.*
>
>*The MAN leaves. JANICE stands frozen, staring away from GOYDA, who rises slowly, painfully, to his feet.*

JANICE: *coldly*
I don't know what you're talking about. . . . I'm not interested.

GOYDA:
That's fine. So long's you remember that you heard it all before once.

JANICE:
If you get the church, you plan to lease it all for yourself?

>*GOYDA stares at her, surprised.*

GOYDA:
I certainly wasn't planning to invite the congregation back, if that's what you're asking.

JANICE:
> You've been bent over that table a long time . . . withdrawn, embittered . . . trying to convince yourself and Irma there's some great value in diligence. She's probably convinced of that herself. . . . Irma convinces easily.

GOYDA: *darkly*
> Leave Irma alone. The last thing she needs is you riding her back.

JANICE:
> I could help you . . . turn your shop in the church into something of a tourist fixture in town with regular stories and photo coverage around the shop and around yourself. But only if you stop thinking selfishly.

GOYDA: *staring at her*
> What in hell are you talking about?

JANICE:
> There are people I know in town who work in coloured glass . . . macramé. . . . Two kids I know would like a place to set up a bakery . . . for production and sale of whole-grain breads. Then there's a couple who would come back to build a vegetarian kitchen!

GOYDA: *angrily*
> Oh, sure . . . hangers-on . . . wilted apple merchants . . . incense-burners . . . all the screwed-over offsprings of the affluent middle class searching for voluntary poverty! Out!

JANICE:
> You're a weak, selfish man!

GOYDA:
> Out!

JANICE:
> You're a cop-out . . . a self-seeker . . . a prick!

She leaves. GOYDA picks up some leatherwork and tries to hand-stitch it. He drives a needle into his finger and sucks on it.

GOYDA:
> Goddammit!

The lights go out on GOYDA's area.

The lights come up on KIOSK talking angrily on the telephone.

KIOSK:
> Yeah . . . well, why put it on the agenda at all? . . . Listen, Homer, your job as town clerk is to work for me an' members of council . . . an' we've got enough to do without goin' over this thing another time! Eh? . . . What in hell makes you think *that*? . . . Then screw your union. When I decide to get rid of you . . . or anyone else in the front office, I'll get rid of you! You think so, eh? . . . Don't push it, alright? . . . That letter from Goyda doesn't go on the council agenda this week. . . . Alright, so it's from my daughter . . . it doesn't go! . . . You've what? . . . Copied an' sent it out already? . . . That does it, Homer . . . you'll be back in the lumberyard countin' two-by-fours for a living!

He slams down the telephone angrily. He then punches the intercom and yells into it.

> Front office! . . . Who's the municipal lawyer?

He waits for a reply which doesn't come. The intercom only burps and crackles back at him.

> Front office? You deaf? . . . It's the mayor here!

37

He gives up on the intercom and leans back in his chair, glowering.

KIOSK:
    Bitch has turned the machine off . . . stands in the window watching the big boys in the school grounds playing football . . . towels bundled up on their crotches so they look like what they got there could hang on a stallion! . . . I've seen her do that . . . her mouth open . . . eyes glassy. . . . It's the vitamins that do it . . . too many vitamins while they're growin' up!

    He rises and prepares to leave the office.

    JANICE enters. For a moment, he doesn't see her. When he does, he is startled by her presence.

Did I have an appointment with you, Webber? . . . I don't remember having an appointment with the press!

JANICE: *laughing*
    For a novice in office, you're taking yourself altogether too seriously, chum.

KIOSK:
    The proper address for a mayor during business hours is "Your Worship" . . . not "chum."

JANICE: *curtsying mockingly*
    Yes, Your Worship! I'm sorry, Your Worship! May I have a word with Your Worship?

KIOSK:
    Cut it out . . . I've got serious problems to consider. This office is not a circus!

JANICE:
> You wanted to be worshipped. . . . How shall I worship an eight-vote lead . . . on one knee, or on two?

KIOSK:
> Bitch! . . . Same as your mother!

JANICE:
> Watch it, Kiosk!

KIOSK:
> Your mother, the accountant! Well, let me tell you, I once took my farm accounts to her an' ended up paying three hundred dollars tax on income I never made!

JANICE:
> I work for a one-woman newspaper. You push it far enough and I'll tighten the vice on your balls until you cry uncle!

KIOSK: *startled, dismayed*
> Shame on you, talkin' like that to a man old enough to be your father! Have you no shame, girl?

JANICE:
> None whatsoever.

> *KIOSK sighs deeply and sits on the edge of his desk.*

KIOSK:
> Did Dolan send you here to queer me around, or you doin' it on your own?

JANICE:
> I find my own stories. . . . For next week's paper, I want to write a history of an old church. I know all about Goyda's wish to turn it into a craft centre.

KIOSK:
>You talked to him. . . . He sent you!

JANICE:
>Yes, I talked to him. But he didn't send me anywhere. Why did you destroy his teaching career?

KIOSK:
>That's crap. He could've gone someplace else to teach.

JANICE:
>He couldn't, an' you know it.

KIOSK:
>Alright, I'll tell you. A man serves the company or employer who pays his wages. Men don't vote if they should go to war . . . no more than they have a right to vote if they should go to work. I'll never quarrel with that, otherwise, nothing would get done. I was chairman of the school board when he sued the board . . . and won. Keeping a man like that around is a poor example to other teachers. . . . I did what I had to do.

JANICE:
>Even when he's right, and you wrong?

KIOSK:
>Even then.

>*She stares at him.*

JANICE:
>You know something? . . . You're more of an ignornant bastard than I first though you were.

>*KIOSK turns his back on her and picks up his papers, preparatory to leaving.*

The lights go out on KIOSK's office.

The lights come up on GOYDA seated, his feet on his table, a bottle of beer in his hand. IRMA sits on the table opposite him. She is excited.

IRMA:
    I've been asking people all over town. . . . Nobody objects. One older woman said a church is a bit like a crafts centre anyway.

GOYDA:
    The opinions of ten people don't matter. This is a village . . . suffering a bad case of time-warp.

IRMA:
    The aldermen are waiting to see what my dad says. But they were interested . . . every one of them.

GOYDA:
    But they'll have to wait and see. . . . Then they'll vote.

IRMA:
    Yes. It's the right way to do things.

GOYDA:
    Irma, listen to me . . . I once proposed to a parents-teachers meeting that Canadian history should be taught in the local schools. Your father chaired the meeting. . . . He called for a vote on the proposal. . . . People were being asked to *vote* on whether their history should be taught to their children! . . . Twenty parents voted for . . . eighteen against. The issue was tabled to die, because it was too controversial.

IRMA:
    What was wrong with that?

GOYDA:
>We're the only goddammed country in the world where a study of national history is not mandatory in the schools. One day we'll vote ourselves into extinction!

IRMA:
>I don't know anything about politics. . . . It bothers me that people get angry talking about politics.

GOYDA:
>You are your father's daughter . . . right to the finishing line!

>*IRMA bows her head in humiliation.*

IRMA:
>I wish I had money or a job I could go to . . . so I might leave this town. Life is so complicated and confused here.

GOYDA:
>Sorry, baby. I can't help you.

IRMA:
>That's not true. . . . You don't want to!

>*GOYDA looks sadly at her and shrugs.*

>*The lights go out on GOYDA and IRMA.*

>*The lights come up on JANICE at her desk typing. She is humming the theme song from the opening scene of the play. She pauses in her typing as DOLAN speaks.*

DOLAN: *offstage*
>Janice!

JANICE:
>Yes, Mister Dolan?

DOLAN:
>   You've been typing non-stop for forty-nine minutes now. I get suspicious when you're not dodging work by going to the john, or trickling the water fountain.

JANICE:
>   I'm on a good story, Mister Dolan.

DOLAN:
>   Is it going to get us into trouble, Janice?

JANICE:
>   No, Mister Dolan.

>   *DOLAN enters in a wheelchair, his eyes shaded by dark sunglasses. A hat of great age and deformity is on his head. He is blind. JANICE talks to him as if he were still in another room.*

DOLAN:
>   They're building a wheelchair ramp leading into city hall, they tell me. . . . Maybe one day I can ride this thing into the dizzying seats of our town power, eh?

JANICE:
>   Sure, Mister Dolan.

DOLAN:
>   They're not doing it for me . . . they've got two cripples on staff, and a third got elected to council. We're gaining power and influence, Janice. To ride a wheelchair is as politically volatile these days as being an Indian militant!

>   *JANICE smiles.*

>   You seen the ramp yet? Is it steep?

JANICE:
>   Yes, Mister Dolan.

DOLAN:
>Good. Maybe one of those bastards will have a failure of the wrists half way up the ramp. That should bring him down into street traffic at about thirty miles an hour, coming in at right angles to the passing cars. If that don't get him, the concrete wall the other side of the street should do the job. . . . By that time the little buggy . . . if well greased . . . would be doing around forty-five miles an hour. Which might open a job for the young and needy.

JANICE:
>That's very thoughtful of you, Mr. Dolan.

DOLAN: *wheeling himself away*
>I'm through for the day, Janice. You lock up. And don't push too hard, you hear? . . . You'll get where you're going, but wait your turn. You need friends in life, Janice . . . as much as you need enemies.

>*He exits.*

>*JANICE ponders what he has said.*

>*The lights go out slowly.*

Act Two

The light value at the opening of this Act is different. The light is unworldly, the Act a journey into dreams, recollections and projected fears of the major protagonists in the play.

The music at the opening of this Act is reminiscent of the previous theme, but the rhythm and melody of the theme song has changed tempo and pitch. A male voice sings the song.

MAN: *singing*
In our town
The demons crawl
Within the darkness
Of the skull
Like gliding hawks
The shadows fall
At seven hours to sundown . . .
In our town
Seven hours to sundown . . .

KIOSK and GOYDA are in their respective playing areas, but the settings they occupied in Act One are stripped down. Each man is isolated. The lights come up on KIOSK and GOYDA, each in a separate pool of light.

KIOSK:
    One morning, she says to me she wants an automatic washer. . . . What the hell for, I says? . . . We've only got one kid . . . the old wringer machine is good enough.

The GRANDFATHER enters, an old shirt in his hands. He squats down and, with a needle and thread, repairs a tear in the shirt.

GRANDFATHER:
    Damned fertilizer's gone up in price! . . . If we cut back anymore, them carrots is gonna be an inch short!

KIOSK:
    I says to her . . . the old wringer machine's good enough!

GRANDFATHER:
    Jews 'ave set up things so an honest man never gets ahead of the game.

KIOSK:
    I bought her the washer like she wanted. But we had to buy tractor gas on time that year.

IRMA enters GOYDA's playing area. She is nervous.

IRMA:
    I walked. . . . He'd hear the car otherwise. . . . You asked me to come.

GOYDA:
> Autumn's arrived. So early this year, Irma. . . . Yesterday it was still summer. . . . Today, the north wind has started to blow.

IRMA:
> You've lost buttons on your jacket. . . . Did you lose them, or are they in your pockets?

GOYA:
> What the hell's a button? . . . Nothing changes here.

IRMA:
> Things grow an' blossom. . . . People I knew as kids are doing interesting things. Peggy Goddard could never learn to read or write. . . . She's teaching music to children now.

GOYDA:
> Peggy Goddard can't count to five on beat. . . . The incompleteness of it all sits like a dust cloud over the streets and houses.

IRMA:
> You ask for too much.

GOYDA:
> And you . . . ask for so little that what you get means nothing.

IRMA: *suddenly agitated*
> That's not true, Jerry! . . . That's not . . . true.

GOYDA:
> The man in Winnipeg . . .

IRMA:
> . . . had three children.

GOYDA:
> You didn't love him. . . . Nobody loves anymore. . . . They negotiate the best arrangements and then settle into a slow, sullen death.

GRANDFATHER:
> She's gettin' fat . . . sleeps late, boy. I was wrong . . . the kid's not yours. I wonder if old Joe Deerin' himself did it to his daughter?

KIOSK:
> What shall I do, Dad?

GRANDFATHER:
> She stands at the front gate, a rake in her hand. But she's not doin' anything. . . . She's starin' down the road . . . after other men.

KIOSK:
> Maybe if I borrowed some money . . . took her an' Irma on a vacation somewhere . . . like Victoria.

GRANDFATHER:
> You get her in the family way . . . get a boy out of her quick. The land's got to go to someone. . . . Without a boy, there's no more Kiosks left.

KIOSK:
> She asked for ten dollars to pay for a ride in an airplane.

GRANDFATHER:
> My boots need new soles. . . . Two teeth need pullin'.

> *He rises and exits, a forefinger prodding into the side of his mouth.*

GOYDA:
> You didn't love him . . . or else, how could you have left him?

IRMA:
>   I loved him, but he didn't love me. There was bitterness. . . . The children woke up screaming at night.

GOYDA: *disturbed by this*
>   Why do people have children . . . when all they give them is food and nightmares?

IRMA:
>   When I left . . . I came here. I was looking for a place to hide, where I could have time to think and understand . . .

GOYDA:
>   Understand what, Irma?

IRMA:
>   Why I'm not loved. Why I'll never be loved.

>   *GOYDA goes slowly towards her and puts his arm around her. They sit down side by side.*

GOYDA:
>   One rides a glider through life . . . avoiding the dark places and the high places . . . hanging on to the edge of the sun . . . but mostly circling familiar places where it's safer to land when the time comes.

IRMA:
>   Do you think two people can make a life happen . . . no magic . . . no help . . . just two people working to make it happen?

GOYDA:
>   I don't know. I tried once . . . lost . . . and ended up in hospital a week for having tried.

IRMA:
>   Could we . . . try?

GOYDA:

    I don't know, I've become a lot like this town . . . content with very little . . . working to the routine of changing days and seasons.

IRMA:

    Nothing else?

GOYDA:

    My books . . . recordings.

    He laughs.

    Like yourself, I also don't believe I can be loved by anyone!

    The both laugh. The lights go down on them.

KIOSK:

    Blasting powder! I could take any rock around into four pieces with a handful of blasting powder. Men working on a three-foot thick pine stump would call for me. . . . Get Sid Kiosk here with a stick of dynamite, they'd say, an' he'll blow the thing to hell!

    The lights come up on DOLAN in a wheelchair. He is grinning sardonically.

DOLAN:

    You can hear, if you listen, flies walk across the ceiling . . . or mountain storms building two hundred miles away. Sometimes I'm thinking, as I listen at my window to street sounds . . . that one can hear the inner workings of a foolish mind. . . . It sounds like a jar of nuts being tumbled.

KIOSK:
>   Bills always got paid an' every item of earnings an' expenses put in a book. Farm has account books goin' back forty-five years now. . . . Otherwise, how does a man know where he's goin', if he don't know where he's been?

DOLAN:
>   Around the world seventeen times in my lifetime. . . . Been everywhere without going further than four miles from the building where I live and work. I know all about African grass plains . . . can even smell the scorched vegetation if I concentrate. Wrote a small book on Argentina once. . . . It got published in Australia.

KIOSK:
>   When I work with blasting powder, I know the place for everything. My old man wouldn't go near the stuff. . . . It scared him. But not me. . . . They'd call for me on the difficult jobs.

DOLAN:
>   Sports track on a Sunday morning . . . cinders hammered by two hundred pairs of feet . . . odour of sweat . . . runners panting past me where I sat and stared through them . . . beyond them . . . to the creeping edge of the Sahara Desert.

KIOSK:
>   Yes, I belong to the two service clubs. . . . I've got opinions about how things should be done. . . . What? No, I'm not a member of a church. But I took flowers to my mother's grave last summer.

JANICE enters DOLAN's playing area.

DOLAN:
>   Janice?

JANICE:
> Yes, Mister Dolan

KIOSK:
> Had a five dollar order of flowers made up nice, an' I drove down an' put them on her grave. The only other person there that morning was Dolan, sittin' in his chair like he'd been made into a headstone.

DOLAN:
> Kiosk took flowers to the cemetery. I think they were intended for his mother. But he made a mistake . . . put them on Bess Henderson's grave instead.

JANICE:
> Should I report on that, Mister Dolan?

DOLAN:
> How well you write. . . . I listen to your work and it warms the room around me. . . . But I'll lose you, won't I, Janice?

JANICE:
> Where would I go?

DOLAN:
> If you stay, I'll teach you everything. . . . I'll teach you to use words as songs to captivate, enchant. . . . Physical beauty is only transitory, Janice. Don't preoccupy yourself with it. . . . The lasting beauty is in the language of the mind.

JANICE:
> Yes . . . I understand.

KIOSK:
> Hell, I never thought of it . . . but if there's some people who feel I should run, I'll run. . . . Is that right, Dad?

> *He listens. Hearing no reply, he is puzzled.*

DOLAN:
> Good! . . . What you have is also a weapon, Janice. Use it to attack and demolish stupidity!

KIOSK:
> Empty the swimming pool at harvest time! . . . No one should be swimming when there's work to do diggin' out potatoes an' shellin' peas!

JANICE:
> Shall I write something on Bess Henderson's grave?

DOLAN:
> Find your targets first . . . then move slowly forward . . . dismantle their defences . . . give no ground . . . but don't take more than you can handle! It's war, Janice . . . a bloodless war of nerves and talent against the darkness!

KIOSK:
> If I do right, will I be remembered? Will all the bad things that've happened be forgotten?

JANICE:
> Everything they do . . . in public and in private . . . all is game, is it not, Mister Dolan?

DOLAN:
> All are pieces in a game of chess. If you stay, I'll teach you all I know, Janice.

JANICE:
> There's so much to learn.

KIOSK:
> A town is like a farm . . . only bigger!

JANICE:
> But I will!

KIOSK:
>Yes . . . I can an' *will* do it! I'll be mayor. . . . I can do it myself! Nobody's ever goin' to tell me what to do an' how! I'll do it!

DOLAN: *hissing*
>Get him, Janice!

JANICE:
>Yes, Mister Dolan.

>>*The lights go down on DOLAN, JANICE and KIOSK.*

>>*The lights come up on GOYDA and IRMA. She is crying.*

GOYDA:
>It takes time, Irma! Everything takes time!

IRMA:
>How long is that?

GOYDA:
>I don't know. Even with your help, I almost lost it all last month.

IRMA:
>Then what can I do to help?

GOYDA:
>Nothing. I have a style and a pace for doing the work and the marketing. . . . It's nothing I can delegate or share. It's only an instinct.

IRMA:
>What about us?

GOYDA:
>We agreed to try . . . a step at a time . . . starting here. It's still here. I'm sorry, but I can't do it!

IRMA:
>At least you're honest.

GOYDA:
>Will it help you if I said I was insane? . . . That pieces of me are spread over twenty years in twenty different places? . . . Like luggage I'll never go back to recover, there are things I need left with other people whose whereabouts I can't locate?

IRMA:
>It's Marlene and your son, isn't it?

GOYDA:
>Yes . . . goddamn them both!

IRMA:
>But they'll never return, and if they did . . . how will you know them? I'm like my father . . . there's not much to know, an' it's not likely to change!

>*They both laugh.*

>You're not insane, Jerry.

GOYDA:
>Then why am I here? I step outside . . . look down the streets . . . and know this is a forgotten, receding world, yet I stay . . . and the madness of the social and political activity even makes sense.

IRMA:
>My father's running for mayor.

GOYDA:
>I know. He'll win.

IRMA:
>It bothers you.

GOYDA:
>No. Not anymore. It's the way things are done, I guess. I got a collie pup once, and swore off getting involved in such things ever again in the town. The pup got run over by a motorbike . . . and . . . I'm still around.

>*The lights go out on IRMA and GOYDA.*

>*The lights come up on ROSSINI. He is speaking on the telephone.*

ROSSINI:
>Sell you a house, Dolan! . . . No sense you paying rent forever on this place. . . . I'm kind of worried about renting this to you any longer. You've got a lot of hardware an' filled-up filing cabinets . . . building wasn't meant to hold up that much weight . . . floors are sagging . . . the roof line's dipping. . . . Well, Dolan, what the hell difference would it make reducing your rent? Won't make the building stronger, will it now?

>*He laughs.*

>Damn right it won't. . . . Shore it up? I can't get workmen goin' down in the basement to do that. . . . Basement's half full of water! . . . No, let me sell you a house. What? . . . Naw, I won't sell you a place where there's water in the basement. . . . That's why I never put this place up for sale. Got just the place for you. . . . One an' one-half storeys . . . your girl can work up on top, an' your place for workin' and living in would be below. . . . I could get my men to lay a couple of two-by-six stringers out the back door to build you a ramp for your chair. . . . That way you can ride out into the backyard an' do your thinking when the sun's out. . . . Eh? No, there's no trees in the backyard . . . lots of old grass, but it can be burned out. . . . Better that way. . . . You don't want yourself runnin' your wheelchair into a maple

tree, do you? . . . I'll let you have it at a discount . . . a quick sale for cash! . . . No, no, it's not downtown . . . but your girl has a car, she can drive. It's four miles out of town, where the air's clean. . . . Think of it, Dolan, clean air, country livin'. . . . You'll live twenty years longer out there!

> *He listens.*

Don't you say that to me!

> *His face hardens with anger. He hangs up the telephone receiver hard. He exits.*

Goddamn cripples . . . try to do them a favour an' they throw shit in your face!

> *The lights go out on ROSSINI.*

> *The lights come up on KIOSK. He is pacing back and forth irritably.*

KIOSK:
The school board . . . made it on the school board in one try. What a mess I found there . . . you wouldn't believe. They had one teacher on staff . . . a woman called Del. . . . That's a man's name. . . . She wore pants, but she said she was a woman. . . . She worked only an hour an' a half a day teaching painting to small kids. What the hell can a kid that age paint? Desks an' walls is what they painted! Never seen such a mess made of public property. I says to the board, "Either that woman starts workin' for a living, or she can hit the road selling Fuller brushes!" Well, that started it . . . all the lay-abouts on school staff came at me. . . . That was the first time Goyda an' I locked horns.

> *The lights come up on GOYDA. He is cold, distant.*

GOYDA:
> The chairman's a joke . . . an anachronism.

KIOSK:
> A town's like a farm. Anybody crossing the fence or comin' through the gate uses the paths that're there to walk on!

GOYDA:
> Let him start picking off individual teachers, and soon he's running a school that's next to useless.

KIOSK:
> I've taken hell long enough from junk dealers an' smart talkers. The day my old man ordered Williston's lumber truck to turn around an' drive out, the credit limit for our farm got lowered in town. The Chamber of Commerce was against the Kiosks . . . so were the holies on account of my wife leavin', but we made it!

GOYDA:
> If Del gets fired, we sue or we walk out!

KIOSK:
> I talked it over with my old man. . . . He was a tough one! "Get any sonofabitch who's out to get you," he says to me. So I went after Goyda.

GOYDA:
> I stood up for Del. . . . Who's standing up for me? . . . Nobody? . . . Are you sheep? . . . The man's illiterate, a village fool! . . . This is my first contract. . . . I can't afford to be dismissed. . . . What are you afraid of? . . . Ah, the homes and second cars you've bought here! Is that it? . . . Del and I never bought anything.

The lights go out on GOYDA.

The lights come up on DOLAN.

KIOSK:
> I didn't like doin' it.... But the young punk was asking for it right from the start.

DOLAN:
> The man is a threat, Janice ... but hopefully he'll never rise beyond the school board. To do that, one needs to have mastered the ability to read.

KIOSK:
> She liked it those first months when my name and picture was in the paper.... "Sid," she said, "you're flyin' high." "It feels good, don't it?" ... Sure, it felt good! ... One night, we had a ribbon-cutting ceremony to open a two-classroom addition to the school. She'd had a bit to drink that night ... somehow got her green skirt snagged and torn.... Going up the steps to the stage so she could stand beside me, she tripped an' fell, spraining her elbow. I gave her the car keys and told her to drive the old man home.

DOLAN: *singing idly to himself, his face straining with concentration* What shall we do with the drunken sailor? ... What shall we do with the ...

KIOSK:
> I didn't know how much she'd drunk.... I didn't know at all.

DOLAN:
> Kiosk's wife took the car down the road to his carrot farm. At Wilbur's corner, she couldn't manoeuvre the turn because of her sprained elbow. She went off the road and down a sharp incline ... the car striking a hundred-year-old fir tree growing in the field below. She came out of the accident without a scratch. Old Jake Kiosk died ... thrown out through the windshield and impaled on a dead

fir limb. He hung there . . . forehead, hands and
tips of his boots touching the tree . . . his grey hat
still on his head.

KIOSK:
They had to cut the branch off with a chain saw to
get him down. . . . What a goddamned way to go!

DOLAN:
He's a dangerous man, Janice!

KIOSK:
Soon after that, the business with the kite-flyin'
rancher an' her started.

DOLAN:
Study the man . . . find his weaknesses . . . work on
them. . . . Wear him down with ridicule!

KIOSK: *with anguish*
It hurt me . . . seein' her in town . . . having Ella
come for a month or two, then go away . . . knowin'
that at night she was doin' with that bone-headed
rancher, Stark . . . what she did only a half dozen
times with me . . . before she started havin' headaches
an' things.

DOLAN:
He's stupid and frustrated . . . like that paperhanger
in Germany who started it all once before. Hit him,
Janice . . . I'll tell you when to let up!

KIOSK:
Never once did that blind cripple, Dolan, come to
me like a man an' say what was bothering him!
There's others who didn't like me . . . but I knew
why!

DOLAN: *singing*
Put him in a longboat till he's sober. . . . Put him in
a longboat till he's sober . . .

KIOSK:
> His father ran the drugstore.... Teachers were hired to go where they lived, back of the store, to teach the blind little bastard.... At noon, they'd wheel him out front, where he sat in his wheelchair, wrapped in a blanket ... starin' through them black glasses like a zombie into the street! I'd walk past him sometimes, but not often.... He gave me the creeps as a kid.

DOLAN: *calling boyishly*
> Hey, Kiosk ... the left heel on your shoes is worn down.... You're limping!

KIOSK:
> How'd he know that? ... The edge of my left heel *had* broken off.... I'd been digging with a shovel and broken it.... I couldn't wear my farm boots to school ...
>
> > *He calls back loudly, replying to DOLAN's taunt.*
>
> It's better'n what you got, Dolan! At least I got feet that work! My father said you shoulda died!

DOLAN: *laughing grimly*
> He said that, eh? ... He could die for saying that.... I could make him die if I wanted, Dolan! I make people like that die just sitting here!

KIOSK:
> I was afraid.... He was weird ... a hot day ... middle of the day, an' he's wrapped up like that in a woollen blanket saying he could make people die! Kids get scared of such things.

DOLAN:
> I can have a wooden stake driven through your heart.... How does that grab you?

> *KIOSK is visibly shaken.*

KIOSK:
> If I'd hit him, all hell would've broken loose. They had a lot of money.... Everybody said so ... to afford teachers goin' into the house to teach him like they did.

DOLAN: *still shouting*
> Kiosk, what's in your head?

KIOSK:
> Brains, same's everybody's!

DOLAN:
> Not in yours. Yours is a farm turnip. Do you know the chemical composition of a turnip?

KIOSK:
> No.

DOLAN:
> Cut a spot open between your eyes. You'll see for yourself!

> *KIOSK reaches up with his hand and rubs the temples between his eyes.*

KIOSK:
> For five years I never walked down that street when they wheeled him out an' left him on the sidewalk to sun. After that, his folks had him sent to some special school.... People who look like that get crazy, I guess.... I've spoken to lots of people about that an' they all agreed.

> *DOLAN laughs and exits, wheeling his chair off the stage.*

I'm sure cripples like him get a government pension. . . . You'd think gettin' a pension like that would make them obligated to being respectful to those of us doin' all the work an' payin' taxes! . . . At least, it shouldn't give them any rights meddlin' in politics! . . . I said it to him once over the telephone, an' the bastard had the rudeness to laugh an' hang up on me!

The lights go out on KIOSK, looking worried and confused.

The lights come up on GOYDA. IRMA stands forlornly on the outer perimeter of the scene.

IRMA:
He offered to buy all twelve vests. . . . I didn't see anything wrong in discounting them ten percent! You said we needed money.

GOYDA:
They're on sale twelve miles down the road this morning . . . in a chain clothing store . . . at forty percent above our retail price!

IRMA:
What's wrong with what someone else does?

GOYDA:
We're competing against ourselves doing that, Irma! . . . If somebody wants a handmade vest, they have to come here . . . where they'll see matching gloves and bags and belts. I'm not a mill running assembly line products. . . . If I was, then why keep this shop?

IRMA:
I'm sorry. . . . You didn't explain.

GOYDA:
It wasn't your fault. . . . I've got a lot on my mind.

IRMA:
> I could take my things and work at home, if that would help.

GOYDA:
> A few years ago, I was doing very well . . . grossing over twenty thousand a year. And rising. . . . There were people coming around by day at first . . . then by night. Wives of doctors . . . doctors, dentists and architects . . . perfumed, overpaid, jaded people looking for kicks and investments. They were buying Group of Seven sketches, hoping the price on what they bought would rise quickly. . . . They began buying out my stock. Then one day, one of them offers me forty thousand dollars . . . for my name!

IRMA:
> I don't understand.

GOYDA:
> I could put my lable only on items he'd buy . . . which he'd hold a few years and re-sell to his wealthy friends at three times the price. Anything else I made to sell here to street trade was no longer to carry my label! Each year, I was expected to dress out his wife in a new outfit . . . and the wives of his friends.

IRMA:
> But . . . nobody can buy another person's name!

GOYDA:
> Oh, yes, they can. . . . Attached to the forty thousand dollar cheque was a four page contract. . . . If I signed it, I sold everything . . . what talents I have . . . my name . . . my reputation . . . even what I said privately or publicly. It was servitude for the rest of my life! . . . Irma, I grabbed a chair and smashed it over the back of that man. He sued. . . . I had to pay for his broken glasses and for assaulting

him. I let my hair and beard grow . . . and I've remained anonymous behind my mask ever since. I don't trust people anymore, honey!

IRMA:
I'll . . . put some coffee on.

GOYDA:
I wanted to see my son after that. . . . Stephen's nine years old then. . . . I wrote a letter to his mother, then drove out to a remote, Godforsaken little valley between two ranges of towering mountains which almost met overhead.

The MAN appears on the periphery of the scene, opposite IRMA. He has a rifle in his hands.

MAN:
I told you long ago to stay away. . . . You remember that? . . . The devil's not welcome into the family.

GOYDA:
He met me at the entrance to the small farm. . . . It was fortified with walls of piled and broken stones. . . . Beyond it, in a small field, children and women were bent to the ground, tilling the gravelley soil with their bare hands. . . . Goats had eaten all the bark and foliage off surrounding trees and stood bleating on outcrops of rock, their eyes wild . . . stomachs distended with hunger . . .

The sound of bleating goats is heard.

MAN:
There's an aura of the devil around you, buddy. . . . So turn around an' keep walkin'.

GOYDA:
>The women and kids were pale and thin. . . . One or two of them looked up at me, but they didn't see me . . . their eyes were dead . . . lips dry and crusted with blood.

MAN:
>Why don't you say somethin' to me? . . . You never say nothin' . . . treat me like I wasn't here! You can't keep doin' that or God will get you!

GOYDA:
>The day was hot, but a cold sweat started trickling down my face. . . . It smelled like ammonia around my face.

>*With a sudden motion, GOYDA whips out his elbow into the face of the MAN, who ducks and strikes GOYDA in the back with the gun butt. GOYDA rises, gasping for breath. The MAN places the gun barrel to the back of GOYDA's head.*

MAN: *speaking quickly, excitedly*
>In your eyes I seen somethin' I seen in the eyes of others before they come here. . . . But you've got the wrong aura. . . . You can't stay. You're lucky for that . . . that there's still hope for you . . . or I'd of killed you like I done two others who come around here from the devil, tryin' to make trouble. . . . You get out of here. . . . You come back when you can talk to me. . . . When you can ask to join the family. . . . When the devil's gone from your heart. . . . You hear me? . . . Now git!

>*The MAN pushes his gun hard against the back of GOYDA's head. GOYDA falls down. The MAN retreats from the scene. IRMA comes up to GOYDA and shakes him.*

IRMA:
> Jerry, wake up! You've slept here all night with your clothes on. I've brought a thermos of coffee. ... Wake up!

GOYDA: *rising slowly, painfully*
> For Christ's sake, stop being a missionary, Irma! I've never cared for missionaries.

> *The lights go out on the scene.*

Act Three

The lights come up slowly on KIOSK and ROSSINI standing in an animated, soundless discussion.

There is the sound of a drum and harmonica played in a driving rhythm. JANICE sings offstage, possibly with other voices.

JANICE: *singing offstage*
    In our town
    The houses stand
    Back to back
    On squares of land
    One in front
    An' two at hand
    At seven hours to sundown . . .
    In our town
    Seven hours to sundown . . .

    There is a drum and harmonica interlude before the next stanza.

JANICE:
> In our town
> The lines are drawn
> No fight is lost
> And none is won
> Each mother wants
> Her neighbour's son
> At seven hours to sundown . . .
> In our town
> Seven hours to sundown . . .

> *The music and song die abruptly as ROSSINI speaks.*

ROSSINI:
> Then learn to keep your mouth shut!

KIOSK:
> Don't you talk to me like that!

ROSSINI:
> I didn't get to own half the town by being a nice guy. If I had to, I'd get your land . . . same way another man got your wife. Kiosk, you're a walking failure . . . a joke . . . a self-righteous buffoon. So is Goyda. . . . The old church is only a piece of vacant real estate. . . . The land the building stands on can be sold. The church is nothing to the rest of us . . . but for you . . .

KIOSK: *breaking*
> Why are you doin' this to me? . . . What have I ever done to hurt you?

ROSSINI:
> Nothing. . . . I'm only trying to tell you, Sid . . . that politics, like finance, is a cold-blooded art. You're not equipped . . . you're makin' mistakes.

KIOSK:
>What mistake have I made?

ROSSINI:
>Running for mayor . . . and winning.

KIOSK:
>An' why not? . . . I was born here! I believe in this town. I want to leave something of myself . . . a plaque on a new building . . . some kind of reputation. I haven't exactly gone anywhere in my life. Now my kid's back to stay. A few years from now, she's gonna marry someone . . . badly. The same thing repeating itself.

ROSSINI:
>That's another mistake . . . passion.

KIOSK:
>But I believe . . . an' I want things for myself and others.

ROSSINI:
>Fine, but don't go showing it! You'd of made a good alderman, Sid. But as mayor, you're in trouble. So don't count on support if it means getting the rest of us in trouble. Otherwise, the council will vote you down . . . and when that happens . . .

KIOSK:
>Are you threatening me, Rossini?

ROSSINI:
>I'm the only friend you have, don't you realize that?

KIOSK:
>You're a goddamned sneaky little Italian!

ROSSINI: *coldly*
>I could break your back for that . . . turn all your little dreams into so much crap.

KIOSK:
> Okay, I'm sorry I said that, but you pushed me!

ROSSINI:
> I could buy and sell you three times over! . . . I can do that with anybody on this council . . . so why in hell do I come into your office when nobody else does? Because I'm your friend. You lose that an' you might as well resign, buddy, because you'll only get what we allow you. Is that understood?

> *KIOSK shakes his head feebly.*

KIOSK: *quietly*
> Yeh . . . I understand.

> *The lights go out on KIOSK and ROSSINI.*

> *The lights come up on GOYDA, IRMA and JANICE.*

IRMA: *speaking to JANICE*
> I'm not interested in what they do at city hall. All I want is to move this shop out to where we'll have more space!

JANICE:
> Then why haven't they accepted Jerry's application?

GOYDA:
> The same reason a pothole in the street takes a year to repair . . . nobody gives a damn, and the one person who could move that procedure along doesn't like me.

JANICE:
> You did wrong, you know. The way to have gone about it was to visit each alderman and discuss your plans before writing an application for lease. They like to feel wise and important . . . and since you're

not exactly a favourite of any of them, they would've appreciated the opportunity to give you hell . . . see you crawl a little.

GOYDA:
>Who in hell's been laying that crap on you . . . Sid Kiosk?

JANICE:
>I know what goes on. . . . I've covered more council meetings than I care to remember. There are two ways of getting city council decisions quickly . . . go in like gangbusters or crawl.

GOYDA:
>Sorry, Janice . . . I do it my way or not at all.

JANICE:
>Fine. But you're in a fight whether you like it or not. So you'd better plan your next step or start looking silly. I've run a story on your problems in today's paper.

GOYDA:
>Who asked you to do that?

IRMA:
>We both thought it would be a good idea if people knew.

JANICE:
>The next step is to increase public interest . . . get more people involved.

GOYDA:
>Involved in what?

JANICE:
>An organization . . . a society for setting up a new crafts centre in town . . . in a vacant, civically owned building!

GOYDA:
> What has this got to do with this shop? If I was in the business of selling hamburgers, I'd be interested in the best shop deal I could get . . . but I wouldn't be inviting the fried chicken place to come in with me!

IRMA:
> You're being difficult, Jerry.

> *GOYDA laughs and throws up his arms.*

> I think Janice is right . . . we should get up an organization, with Jerry as chairman. You could be the secretary, Janice.

JANICE:
> I can't be signing letters, then reporting on them for the paper. My boss can sympathize with many paradoxes, but not that one.

IRMA:
> Then I'll be secretary. You be the treasurer.

GOYDA:
> In case you two have forgotten, I own a controlling interest in this shop!

JANICE:
> You're such a dear when you're cooperative, but a bastard when you put your mind to it. . . . This is in your best interest. The three of us leading an organization can put them back on their ears.

GOYDA:
> Three of us . . . with equal voting power?

IRMA:
> Of course.

JANICE: *sweetly*
> I'm sure we'll never disagree.

GOYDA: *sarcastically*
　　I'm sure we never will!

IRMA:
　　It's settled then? We can call ourselves the Crafts Centre Committee.

JANICE:
　　Fine. I'll look into getting a charter. Jerry doesn't follow through on his application. *We* go after a lease on the old church, right?

GOYDA: *speaking to IRMA*
　　Do you really know what you're doing?

IRMA:
　　Janice wants to help. I'm sure my father will be happier dealing with an organization. . . . It won't hurt his pride. I think it's time we started considering the community more. . . . This shop was a good beginning . . . but . . . it looks and feels like . . . it's old . . . dying.

GOYDA:
　　I go along or I buy you out, is that it?

IRMA:
　　I'm afraid so, Jerry.

　　　　The lights go out on them.

　　　　The lights come up on KIOSK and ROSSINI. KIOSK is now confident; ROSSINI, upset.

KIOSK:
　　A *what*?

ROSSINI:
>A crafts committee, but it's the same bunch . . . your daughter, Goyda and our friend at the newspaper. On top of that, I get a lease termination notice from Goyda, effective in sixty days.

KIOSK:
>Evict him tomorrow. I'd do that!

ROSSINI:
>If he's going, I'll need sixty days to find someone new for the building. If this is something Goyda has figured out, why didn't he do it before?

KIOSK:
>He's capable of anything . . . an' he's bound to take my girl with him. I've said no to him already . . . I'm not backing down to his tricks.

ROSSINI:
>Town secretary has duplicated and sent the new application to all the aldermen.

KIOSK:
>What does it take to fire that Homer?

ROSSINI:
>He's doing what he's been hired to do.

KIOSK:
>How are you treating this . . . this new application when it comes up on the council agenda?

ROSSINI:
>I'm losing Goyda's lease. . . . I don't like it, but he's in his rights. . . . If he gets the church, I'm out of rent, but . . .

KIOSK:
>You'll vote to let him lease?

ROSSINI:
> Why not?

KIOSK:
> Sure . . . why not? He hasn't got a home or obligations to this town. . . . People build a church an' he gets it for the asking. Times get rough an' he'll go on welfare . . . so would my daughter. . . . There's no pride left. Is that what property owners elected us to do? Other men *build* new buildings for their businesses.

ROSSINI:
> He asks for a lease, not expropriation.

KIOSK:
> I don't trust people who own nothing . . . they have a thirty-day outlook on everythin' they rent. . . . We have to look after the years for better or worse. Why is it that way? . . . Who says it has to be like that?

ROSSINI:
> I never thought of it. All the same, it works.

KIOSK:
> So does Communism.

ROSSINI:
> Well, I have an idea . . . you may not like it, but it may save me rent loss and give you peaceful sleep by spreading responsibilities around a bit.

> *The lights to out on KIOSK and ROSSINI.*

> *The lights come up on JANICE who is at her desk preparing newspaper layouts.*

DOLAN: *singing offstage*
> What shall we do with the drunken sailor?
> What shall we do with the drunken sailor?
> What shall we do with the drunken sailor? . . .

He calls loudly, so that JANICE can hear

DOLAN:
Ask Constable Radomsky to apprehend his driving licence before he drives into a light pole, that's what we do. . . . Janice?

JANICE:
I'm here.

DOLAN:
How many obituaries are going into this week's paper?

JANICE:
Three . . . two old-timers and Jimmy Hessler, who drowned.

DOLAN:
And how many help wanteds have we got?

JANICE:
One . . . for a part-time bricklayer's helper. . . . Why?

DOLAN:
Just wanted to know how the town economy was doing.

He laughs offstage. JANICE laughs with him and continues working.

The lights come up on the remaining areas of the stage.

KIOSK is at his desk, squinting at the paper work before him.

GOYDA is also examining some papers. He dials a number on his telephone. The telephone on KIOSK's desk rings. GOYDA gets a busy signal and hangs up.

KIOSK: *officiously*
    Hullo. . . . No, this is not Hogarth's Welding. . . . This is the mayor's office! . . . No, I'm not kidding. . . . Who in hell are you?

    His caller hangs up as GOYDA dials again. KIOSK drops the telephone down hard and scowls. The telephone immediately rings again.

    Why don't they leave me alone?

    He answers the telephone.

    Hullo!

GOYDA:
    This is Jerry Goyda calling, Mr. Mayor.

KIOSK: *surprised*
    Yeah . . . well . . . how you doin', kid?

GOYDA:
    I'm calling about . . .

KIOSK: *speaking officiously, the mayor now*
    Well, council decided to table your request, boy. We felt we needed more information.

GOYDA:
    Information about what?

KIOSK:
    Information . . . that's all. Listen . . . did you call this number just a moment ago?

GOYDA:
    No, I didn't. . . . How was the council decision arrived at, sir?

KIOSK:
    Why do you wanna know?

GOYDA:
>The newspaper report on council meeting made no mention of a discussion on my proposal.

KIOSK:
>Who was there to discuss with? You didn't appear before us. . . . Anyway, things like that are decided in committee now.

GOYDA:
>I've given my rental termination to Mr. Rossini. . . . I didn't see any difficulty acquiring a lease on the old church . . . yet . . .

KIOSK:
>You shouldn't count your chicks before they're hatched, should you? ·

GOYDA:
>What further information is it you need?

KIOSK:
>Something more on the nature of . . . your . . . what you call it? Committee? I never heard of that before. Your ability to pay . . . an' all the rest of it.

GOYDA: *angrily*
>Dammit, I've been around long enough to be known in the community!

KIOSK: *trapping him*
>Ah . . . for me . . . no! But there's other members on council who never go near a shop like yours. They might see the old church being reduced to a flophouse an' then abandoned. You've got to see other points of view, Goyda.

GOYDA:
>Nobody on council has a right to feel that way!

KIOSK:
> I agree, but life is life, boy. We need a . . . a feasibility report on the state of . . . the mechanical condition of the building. Who knows what shape's the roof in . . . or if the wiring won't burn out!

GOYDA:
> I'd have to hire a professional engineer for that . . . and that costs money. Since town hall is the landlord in this case, would you be prepared . . .

KIOSK:
> Nope . . . I don't see why we have to pay when it's you who wants the building. As it is, I don't think the building's worth anything. The land it stands on should of been sold off by the previous administration to offset municipal operating costs. They should of done that, if they'd been worth a damn . . . which they weren't . . . but that's between you an' me.

GOYDA:
> I'll see about preparing a report on the condition of the building. Would this mean the building is available to me if the report is favourable?

KIOSK:
> As far as I'm concerned, you could move in today. It's the others who are worried.

GOYDA:
> Yeh . . .

> *They both hang up their telephones. KIOSK jiggles the telephone cradle.*

KIOSK:
>Marge? . . . Give me the building inspector . . . quick! . . . Joe? It's me. What's with the heating system at the old church? . . . It's totally dependent on the furnace in the parish hall? . . . Good! . . . An' the guys with the funny hats still got a lease on that building? . . . Thanks. . . . Oh, nothing. . . . I just wanted to know.

>*During the last speech, JANICE collects her papers and goes to GOYDA's area of the set. IRMA enters to join them.*

>*The lights go out slowly on KIOSK.*

GOYDA: *looking with surprise at the papers that JANICE gives him* Forty members? . . . There actually *is* an organization!

JANICE:
>Sure. You ask people to sign up and they sign up.

GOYDA:
>But . . . at least a dozen of these people have nothing to do with crafts in this community. I know everybody who's active. . . . These people aren't.

JANICE:
>You're not the craft centre, Jerry. What form a centre takes is up to the membership.

>*GOYDA stares at JANICE, then at IRMA, who looks away.*

GOYDA:
>I am supposed . . . to have my work and livelihood left to the decision of outside people . . . who've got no experience or understanding of what I do . . . or how . . . or even why? Every organization I've ever

belonged to reserved the right to accept or reject membership applications. . . . Who are these people? What am I chairman of?

> IRMA is hurt and moves away. JANICE becomes annoyed.

JANICE:
We have an objective to accomplish. . . . We need people . . . numbers of people!

GOYDA:
Not this way. . . . No way!

JANICE:
There is no other way!

GOYDA:
On two occasions in the past, I've come within an inch of losing this place and all inventory. It was my knowing what to do . . . and doing it . . . that saved me from closing down.

IRMA:
This shop is only a small part of it, Jerry!

GOYDA: *rising to his feet, facing them*
This shop . . . my work . . . is it supposed to catalyst something else? Is there something you haven't told me?

> They do not reply.

I'm asking you?

> He speaks to IRMA.

You've invested some money and a lot of voluntary work. . . . I've got twenty thousand dollars in here!

IRMA:
> As Janice says, this should only be a small part of the project.

GOYDA:
> There is no project . . . there's only my application for a lease. . . . I'm applying for a lease of the church for this shop. . . . Period!

JANICE:
> Other people have other plans for the building.

GOYDA:
> Then take your non-existent people and plans and get yourselves out of here so I can get on with what I'm doing!

IRMA:
> I don't like hearing that from you!

GOYDA:
> Fine. . . . I'll buy you out and find someone else to help!

JANICE:
> You had helpers once before . . . two stand out in my mind. Roger, who stole leather and polished stones . . . and Nick, the alcoholic. . . . They brought on the first of your two crises. . . . Right?

GOYDA:
> I don't think that's any concern of yours, Janice.

JANICE:
> Irma and I have done a lot for this community . . . and for you. Any change now is not going to be only a change in location. There's got to be a change in attitudes.

GOYDA:
> What does that mean?

JANICE:
> Group decisions on everything.

GOYDA:
> Ah, the workers taking over the factory! You're welcome to it . . . the tools, the supplies . . . the accounts payable which, when paid . . . would leave me with earnings of one hundred and eight dollars for this month!

IRMA:
> That's not what Janice said, Jerry.

GOYDA:
> Good . . . from now on she doesn't interfere with my work, or I with hers!

JANICE: *considering the situation*
> Either we agree as a committee, or this shop's application for a lease on the church is not the only one going to town council.

GOYDA:
> You . . .

JANICE:
> Yes.

> *GOYDA smiles coldly and sits down in exasperation.*

GOYDA:
> I see . . . I pay the rent. In a week, you're baking unchewable bread to sell on the doorstep. . . . Then comes the hookah pipe carvers with shaven heads.

JANICE: *angry*
> Do you want a vote now . . . here? Or shall we call a membership meeting? . . . In both places you'd lose out, and you know it!

The lights go out on GOYDA's shop.

The lights come up on KIOSK's office. KIOSK and ROSSINI are seated on the same side of the desk.

KIOSK:
    They're comin'?

ROSSINI:
    They asked to come. You let me handle this . . . you tend to lose your temper quickly.

KIOSK:
    Me? . . . What in hell you talking about?

ROSSINI:
    That's fine . . . just keep your voice down. Everything's alright.

    GOYDA, IRMA and JANICE enter.

    ROSSINI is expansive, smiling.

    Ah, representatives from the Crafts Centre Committee, Your Worship! Come on in!

KIOSK: *under his breath*
    Shit!

ROSSINI:
    His Worship and I are pleased to receive you on behalf of town government.

KIOSK:
    Get on with it, Rossini . . . I've got an appointment with the dentist.

ROSSINI:
    We've examined your feasibility study carefully and wonder how your technical findings were made?

GOYDA:
> We employed the services of a mechanical engineer. If you'd read the report, his signature appears at the end of the findings!
>
> *JANICE grins and begins writing.*
>
> *Both KIOSK and ROSSINI turn to the last pages of the report before them. KIOSK glances up and stares at JANICE.*

KIOSK:
> What's she writing there? You came to talk, not to write!

JANICE:
> I'm here as a news reporter, Mr. Mayor. This interview is being covered by the press. Is there some objection? Or a new regulation prohibiting me from doing what I'm employed to do?

KIOSK:
> Goddammit, but you can't take a crap anymore without the press being around!
>
> *He turns and speaks to ROSSINI.*
>
> Does she have to be here?

ROSSINI:
> Everything we do is public, Your Worship . . . even the thing you just mentioned.
>
> *He grins at his joke.*
>
> I see no reason why she can't report on this meeting.
>
> *KIOSK loosens his tie angrily.*

KIOSK: *speaking to the delegation*
> Alright . . . what else?

GOYDA: *staring him down*
>We *did* have an appointment, did we not? If so, why are we being met with this hostility?

KIOSK:
>What in blue tarnation do you expect . . .

ROSSINI: *cutting in*
>No, Mr. Goyda, there's no hostility. Both the mayor and myself, as chairman of the public buildings committee, are delighted you were able to come . . . accompanied by your friends. Now . . .

GOYDA:
>Do we, or do we not, get a lease on the old church?

ROSSINI:
>Nothing can be rushed. . . . I must say you provided a thorough report on the condition of the building. However, I'd question some details of the findings . . . such as the condition of the roof. Young Billy Myers climbed up the attic to ring the bell last summer, when he had no right being there. . . . When the firemen got him down, he said he'd seen through the shingles of the roof.

GOYDA:
>A divine revelation . . .

ROSSINI:
>What?

>*The women laugh.*

GOYDA:
>Young Billy Myers is doing two years for car theft. We didn't consult with him. We consulted with a mechanical engineer!

ROSSINI:
>The point is well taken. . . . Now, the electrical wiring . . .

GOYDA:
>Again, we're not applying to establish an electrified cement mixing plant. You requested a report on whether the building was serviceable for our purposes. If you'd read the report, you'd find the answer is affirmative.

>>*ROSSINI is becoming visibly unsure of himself. He keeps his temper in check but his speech is becoming more rapid.*

ROSSINI:
>Parking . . . there's only room for thirty cars in the lot, it says here.

KIOSK:
>I'm not allowin' any street parking from now on except if the building re-opens as a church.

IRMA:
>But Dad . . .

GOYDA: *cutting in*
>Again, thirty parking spaces are more than adequate. If not, there's a supermarket parking lot within two blocks.

KIOSK: *eagerly*
>That's private property. You're not leasing the supermarket parking lot!

>>*He turns and speaks to ROSSINI.*

>Tell them an' let's get it over with.

IRMA:
>Tell us what? Can someone please explain why this meeting feels like a fire fight?
>
>*KIOSK is distressed.*

ROSSINI:
>We see the merits of your proposal...
>
>*He turns to scowl at KIOSK.*
>
>...but unfortunately...

GOYDA:
>We don't get the lease!

ROSSINI:
>There's no heating for it, Jerry. As landlords, we can't rent a building without heating facilities.

GOYDA:
>The one I rented from you got around that one.
>
>*ROSSINI bites back his anger.*
>
>The furnace to the church is in the parish hall.

ROSSINI: *his voice rising*
>True, in the parish hall, but not the church. The hall is leased by someone else.

GOYDA:
>They never use the place. The heat can be left on and billed to us.

ROSSINI:
>No, it's against municipal building by-laws.

GOYDA:
>Then arrange for a waiver, for God's sake. This is not a federal constitutional question!

JANICE: *muttering*
>That's a good lead line for the story.

KIOSK: *exploding*
>Screw your story, lady!

GOYDA:
>I protest! His Worship made an abusive remark. We are members of a responsible organization and we demand an apology.

KIOSK:
>No bloody way, boy.

ROSSINI:
>Young man, you are also being abusive. Yesterday you make up an organization and today we're called upon to apologize for things said in dispute.... Do you think yourselves equal to the Chamber of Commerce?

GOYDA:
>As a member of that organization as well, I can ask the Chamber to respond to your question, if you wish.

ROSSINI:
>I'm sorry ...

IRMA:
>Please ... can't we just talk this over like civilized human beings?

ROSSINI: *addressing Irma*
>I can only apologize.

>*He turns and speaks to GOYDA.*

ROSSINI:
> No, you can't have the old church. Nobody can have it. The committee of which I'm chairman reviewed your request, and we've decided to propose to council the building be demolished and the land on which it stands sold to pay off municipal debentures.
>
> *There is a stunned silence. JANICE slowly raises her hand.*
>
> Yes . . .

JANICE:
> Has council already voted . . . or decided in committee that the old church is to be demolished?

KIOSK:
> Hell, no . . . but they will.

JANICE:
> They will?

KIOSK:
> You're damned right they will! Who's runnin' this town, you? Or I?

JANICE:
> Thank you, Your Worship.
>
> *She rises quickly and leaves. ROSSINI watches her go. He is worried.*

ROSSINI: *addressing KIOSK*
> I think you'd better phone the publisher of the paper and get that story straight.

GODYA:
> That's fast thinking, Alderman!

ROSSINI: *impatiently*
> Alright, the meeting's over.

> *IRMA and GODYA leave. ROSSINI paces back and forth in the office area.*

KIOSK:
> Relax. . . . I wonder what makes my daughter get involved with characters like that?

ROSSINI:
> Never mind your daughter. . . . One of two things had better be done fast, Kiosk.

KIOSK:
> Like what?

ROSSINI:
> Like you get on that telephone and call the others with a deal to close ranks around you . . . promise them your vote on their pet hang-ups . . . anything. Or you get ready to resign and get your ass out of municipal politics for good in this town!

KIOSK:
> Who in hell you think you're talkin' to, Rossini?

ROSSINI:
> If I know Goyda and his two lady helpers, we're in trouble . . . bad trouble.

> *The lights go out on KIOSK and ROSSINI, with KIOSK staring vacantly at ROSSINI.*

> *The lights come up on GOYDA's shop. GOYDA is at his workbench. IRMA is folding handbills at the other end of the table. JANICE is preparing to interview GOYDA for a radio show. She checks her cassette tape recorder and holds the microphone before his face.*

GOYDA:
>Come on, Jan. . . . This is ridiculous.

JANICE:
>People need information . . . they're demanding it. Trust me.
>
>*She adopts a radio voice.*
>
>Mr. Goyda . . . you operate a crafts shop in Woodlands, is that true?

GOYDA:
>Yes.

JANICE:
>And how long have you done this?

GOYDA:
>For six years, and some years prior to that on a part-time basis.

JANICE:
>You were also a founding member of the Woodlands Crafts Centre Committee . . . an organization of concerned and responsible people. What is your role presently in this commitee?

GOYDA:
>I'm the interim chairman.

JANICE:
>It is widely recognized that you have contributed much to this community in exhibits and crafts development . . .
>
>*GOYDA grimaces at her. She ignores him.*
>
>Your recent decision to revitalize a historic community building now vacant and neglected is also drawing wide community support.

GOYDA:
>That's a question I'm not prepared to . . .

>*He motions with his hand to cut the interview. She ignores him.*

JANICE:
>Concerned people in Woodlands are now looking to you and your committee as standing between the first church built in this town . . . and the demolition hammer threatening it now as a result of city hall decisions!

GOYDA: *sharply*
>The decision to demolish this building was arrogant and came as a surprise, but . . .

JANICE: *closing hard on him*
>You went before the mayor and representatives of council to argue for saving a historic building. What was their response for an alternative plan of renovation and public use?

GOYDA:
>I never argued for saving the church . . . merely for leasing it to us as a crafts centre! The decision to demolish was announced at my last meeting with them.

JANICE: *feigning surprise*
>You had no previous indication of this decision?

GOYDA: *with exasperation*
>Yes! Look, I don't care if they turned the place into a hamburger take-out business!

JANICE:
>Yes, your anger is understandable. . . . You were informed at this last meeting with the mayor of a plan to demolish the historic church and sell the land it occupies for development, is that right?

GOYDA:
>The question of development didn't come up.

JANICE:
>But one can assume that was the intention of the Woodlands civic government.

GOYDA:
>One can assume anything, I suppose.

JANICE:
>Thank you. That was Jerry Goyda for evening radio news from Woodlands.

>*The lights go out on the scene with GOYDA.*

>*The lights come up on KIOSK and ROSSINI. ROSSINI is seated, glum. KIOSK is pacing back and forth. The telephone rings. He stares at it, but does not answer it.*

ROSSINI:
>You going to answer it?

KIOSK:
>It's another call like the ones I've been gettin' all morning. Can't we sue that bastard?

ROSSINI:
>I heard the interview. There's nothing we can sue for.

KIOSK:
>Daughter or not, I told Irma to find herself another place to live.... I can't have her around my home now.... My own kid.... When I told her that, she just looked at me like I wasn't there an' said, "You can't see beyond your feet.... I feel sorry for you." What a helluva thing to say to your old man! ... An' Tom, if that bitch from the newspaper ever shows her nose in here, I'm throwin' her out!

ROSSINI:
> You've got to cool down, Sid . . . your health won't take too much of this.

KIOSK:
> There's nothing wrong with my health. . . . I've never felt better.
>
> *Speaking sadly.*
>
> What's happened to respect for public office? It never used to be like this. . . . One disagreement an' they're on the radio making hay of the whole damned business . . . ridiculing, undermining confidence.

ROSSINI:
> Things started off wrong. Positions were too severe. . . . Things from the past got in the way.

KIOSK:
> I thought the older a man gets, the more respect he earns from things he did. . . . It takes a long time. I don't want to be laughed at, Tom.

ROSSINI:
> Neither do I.

KIOSK:
> What do we do now? If you think calling on them . . . asking for another meeting would . . .

ROSSINI: *angrily*
> Do that . . . and sink yourself good! You should've thought of all that before the role of mayor got into your head!

KIOSK: *feeling helpless*
> That doesn't help me. . . . I need someone who knows how to put things together again.

ROSSINI:
: Give an inch now and you can call a new election for mayor! Because if Goyda doesn't . . . that Webber girl will . . . call for your resignation!

KIOSK:
: But not yours?

ROSSINI: *smiling coldly*
: Nope.

KIOSK:
: If I go down, I'm takin' the whole council down with me. . . . You'd better understand that! You all voted on the position I took.

ROSSINI:
: Why not take the whole town, while you're at it? You really can't see beyond your feet, you know.

KIOSK:
: When I was a kid . . . it was the English remittance men an' their kids who did it to us. Next, it'll be you. . . . As a kid, if I invited their kids to my birthday party, they never came. . . . I stood behind trees, watching them . . . a goddamned second-class citizen in my own country. . . . I'm never gonna forget that!

ROSSINI:
: What's it got to do with me? You don't hear me crying about things like that. . . . It doesn't bother Goyda . . . or your daughter. Certainly not the newspaper lady. Nobody cares about the dreams of old men, Kiosk! You pay for what you need, that's all that matters. If you can't pay, that's another thing . . . then you're a bum.

KIOSK:
: They call you the Italian behind your back. You want to be called that all your life?

ROSSINI: *laughing*
>I don't care what in hell they call me. I own more than I can eat . . . putting my kid through university. . . . I've even had enough friends to elect me to town council. So, do I worry? If I was an Indian or a cripple, maybe I'd worry . . . but I'm not.

KIOSK:
>No pride at all, eh? . . . I've got pride, Rossini. I don't take crap from anyone no more . . . not even from my daughter. An' certainly not from an educated bum who can do better things, but goes into a business a woman or somebody with less education could do. He's takin' away someone else's work!

ROSSINI:
>That's his problem. . . . We've got ours.

KIOSK:
>What do we do now?

ROSSINI:
>Council will support you . . . they have to so's not to lose face. We all made a mistake. It doesn't mean much, but we've got to prevent Goyda winning.

KIOSK:
>He won't, then.

ROSSINI:
>He'll win . . . if he's willing to go after us. With that radio interview, he's got the first jump. There's two options open to us.

KIOSK:
>What's that?

ROSSINI:
>	You go on radio . . . be nice . . . but accuse him of making a big issue out of nothing. Make our position look responsible.

KIOSK:
>	I don't like it.

ROSSINI:
>	While you're being reasonable, the rest of us move like hell with a demolition tender . . . find a quick buyer for the church land so it's sold soon's the building's down. Nobody argues long with something that's done and over with . . . because even if we lose the argument, it won't change a thing!

>>	*KIOSK begins to realize what ROSSINI is proposing. He straightens up resolutely.*

KIOSK:
>	Alright . . . if that's the way it has to be then that's the way it is. When I go on radio, what'll I say?

ROSSINI: *rising, facing him coldly*
>	You'll say what your political instincts tell you to say . . . nothing more . . . nothing less. If you don't, you're dead!

>>	*Mechanically, like robots, KIOSK and ROSSINI move from their office to the newspaper office. JANICE, dressed in cold colours, holds up a microphone as they approach. KIOSK goes to the microphone and begins to speak into it.*

KIOSK:
>	My colleagues and I respect the people in the Woodlands Crafts Centre Committee an' welcome all they've done for the community. It's helped to develop an image for our town as a good place to live. But, we are elected to be responsible for problems which the committee has not satisfactorily

helped us resolve. We asked them for hard information on the old church. Much of their information was idealistic. Our own assessment was that . . . regretfully . . . the building is in bad repair and must be demolished for public safety. Should the committee bring a proposal to *build* a new centre for their needs, we'd be more than happy to consider their proposal.

JANICE cuts the mike.

JANICE:
That's the position you're staying with?

KIOSK:
What does it sound like, lady?

KIOSK looks to ROSSINI for approval. ROSSINI is cold and distant, the general on the battlefield. JANICE is a mirror image of ROSSINI.

JANICE:
It sounds like something I've heard elsewhere . . . on other issues. From Alderman Rossini.

KIOSK laughs loudly. He continues laughing as ROSSINI escorts him from the newspaper office to the mayor's office. ROSSINI slaps him across the face. KIOSK blinks, his laughter dying abruptly.

ROSSINI:
Stay with what you said . . . no matter what happens. . . . You repeat what you said over and over. . . . Do you understand?

KIOSK: *woodenly*
Count on me, Tom. You know you can count on me.

During the above exchange, JANICE moves her tape recorder to GOYDA's shop. While JANICE briefs him soundlessly, IRMA paints signs reading "Heritage, Yes — Bulldozers, No!"

DOLAN: *from offstage, in the newspaper office*
Janice? ... Are you there? ... Can you tell me why the only bastards in town who don't subscribe to the paper are coming and going through here like I was a bootlegger in a dry town?

GOYDA: *speaking to JANICE*
Is that all he said?

JANICE:
Yes ... you're on.

GOYDA:
The issue is no longer a dispute between our organization and members of town council. The arrogance of Mayor Kiosk ... the decision to demolish the only building remaining from the original town site ... must be stopped! Our membership is canvassing with petitions. The ministers of three active churches have given us support. Protest posters are available at the leather shop!

The lights come up on KIOSK and ROSSINI who are listening to a radio.

We request the town fathers turn the decision on the church to a citizens' committee for further study and recommendations!

ROSSINI:
Goddamn him!

KIOSK:
Over my dead body!

GOYDA:
>We ask the city council to revoke the demolition order as of today!

ROSSINI: *addressing KIOSK quietly*
>No.

KIOSK: *loudly*
>No!

GOYDA: *angrily*
>We demand members of council come to their senses and stop behaving like village fascists!

ROSSINI AND KIOSK:
>Like hell!

>*KIOSK and ROSSINI huddle in silent conversation. KIOSK dials a number on his telephone and begins a soundless conversation.*

GOYDA: *pushing the microphone away and rising to his feet* How are the petitions doing, Irma?

IRMA: *upset*
>Six hundred signatures. . . . You're after him? You're out to get him, aren't you? This issue is not as important as breaking my father down!

JANICE: *moving towards her*
>Irma . . . you're tired.

IRMA:
>Don't touch me! You're both out to get him! You are moving headstones in a country graveyard . . . dead . . . no feeling . . . no tears . . . no remorse . . . no hope. You're no different than he was! It's just a killing game. . . . Nobody cares for anybody!

>*JANICE turns away from her.*

JANICE: *speaking to GOYDA*
    I'll take her to my place. . . . There's a demonstration being organized around City Hall.

GOYDA: *startled*
    What demonstration? . . . When?

JANICE:
    Friday evening.

IRMA: *in great frustration*
    I'm going by myself! I'm going home. There's nobody left. Everything is dead. Frozen. It was a lie! . . . You both lied to me . . . to yourselves! . . . I'm going home.

> *She runs out of the shop.*
>
> *JANICE and GOYDA look after her, briefly, but their minds are on other things. GOYDA turns on JANICE.*

GOYDA:
    Who in hell gave you authority to do that? We never discussed a demonstration as a tactic!

JANICE:
    I've canvassed some of the members who agreed.

GOYDA:
    What members? . . . There's never been a membership meeting!

JANICE:
    The members I brought into the organization.

GOYDA:
    A public meeting would've been fine . . . but not a demonstration . . . not in this town!

JANICE: *sneering*
> Why not? It's time Woodlands joined the twentieth century along with the rest of the world.

GOYDA:
> I agreed to chair the group. . . . I expect to be consulted before action such as this is considered.

JANICE:
> Listen, baby, you're a shopkeeper. In the end, you'll be influenced by that consideration. The demonstration's on.

> *The telephone rings, as KIOSK hangs up his own phone. JANICE answers the phone.*

> Yes? . . . Great! . . . Bring them in. . . . No, send them over by cab!

> *She hangs up the telephone and turns to GOYDA happily.*

> Petitions have topped one thousand signatures. . . . By tomorrow, more people will have signed than voted for the mayor! You should announce that, Jerry.

GOYDA: *stonily*
> Announce it yourself. . . . Get your bread bakers and prune eaters together and announce it with a bullhorn down Main Street. If you run into the mayor while doing it, you might give him a flower and then break his legs with a club! Get out of here!

> *Ignoring him, she holds up the microphone. She smiles warmly at him.*

JANICE:
> Just make the announcement and then go have yourself a coffee, Jerry.

GOYDA:
> I want you to clear out . . . and stay out of Irma's life as well!

JANICE:
> It's not some diabolical scheme. . . . It's the end of a time in this town. Win or lose, the town fathers will have to reverse gear . . . under pressure.

GOYDA:
> But you won't stop there. . . . No way! The taste of power is too heady for our Janice. . . . No small town paper is going to tie you down *now*!

JANICE:
> Look at it this way then . . . our membership didn't elect you . . . or Irma . . . or me. We elected ourselves . . . to get a new location for Jerry Goyda's shop. It's not quite true, but that's what people will be saying. Pulling back now makes you a mark. . . . Announce the petition results.

GOYDA:
> No.

JANICE: *annoyed now*
> You'll do what has to be done. Just as Kiosk reacts to what he's told to do. . . . Kiosk is nothing . . . a piece of carboard. It's Rossini we're fighting!

GOYDA:
> It's the same over there?

He points in KIOSK's direction.

JANICE:
> Yes.

GOYDA:
>   And I'm . . . also . . . made of cardboard? You knew how it was going . . . right from the start!

>   *JANICE avoids his eyes.*

>   *The lights come up on DOLAN's wheelchair. His phone is off the hook.*

>   *The telephone rings in KIOSK's office. He answers it.*

KIOSK:
>   Yeh . . . speaking. . . . What? . . . When? . . . How bad is it?

>   *KIOSK hangs up the telephone, his face frozen.*

>   *JANICE hangs up DOLAN's phone.*

ROSSINI:
>   Someone find a new pothole in the street?

KIOSK:
>   Irma's car . . . went off the highway overpass . . .

ROSSINI:
>   Is she . . . alright?

>   *KIOSK moans and covers up his face with his hands. ROSSINI rises and goes upstage from him. He stands rigidly, opening and closing his hands.*

GOYDA:
>   If I was to walk out that door and go talk to Kiosk directly . . . explain how both of us were being worked over . . .

JANICE:
>I wouldn't recommend it. It would give him the kind of advantage you'd get if he decided to come here and see you first . . . for the same reason.

GOYDA: *savagely*
>How does the remainder of the scenario read? . . . Let's get it over with so I can see Rossini about recovering my lease before someone else picks it up and I'm out on my ear in the street!

>>*JANICE puts away her microphone and hands a paper to GOYDA. He reads it, then moves to KIOSK's office, followed by JANICE, who takes out her notebook.*

>>*KIOSK drops his hands from his face as GOYDA enters. KIOSK's face is dead, his words wooden and without feeling.*

KIOSK:
>Is it the resignation of council you want? . . . Or mine?

>>*The sound of human voices offstage growing slowly in volume is heard. ROSSINI turns to stand behind KIOSK.*

GOYDA:
>We are not here to waste Your Worship's or our own time. Fourteen hundred signatures on our petition demand a reversal of demolition order on the old church.

>>*GOYDA hands over the sheaf of papers to him. KIOSK ignores them.*

KIOSK:
>Tenders have been given. . . . We have a buyer for the church lots.

GOYDA:
> The petitioners demand a reversal of that decision!

The crowd sounds grow louder.

KIOSK:
> Whatever you want.

GOYDA: *surprised*
> I beg your pardon, sir . . .

KIOSK:
> Tell Rossini what you want, Goyda. . . . Someone will look after it.

The crowd sound becomes a cheer.

ROSSINI: *groping now*
> What His Worship means is that . . . the entire question of your lease application . . . will be reviewed by a committee . . . made up of representatives from our side . . . an' from your side . . . as well as members from the community at large. Is that agreeable?

KIOSK rises and turns away from them.

KIOSK:
> Irma died . . . in her car. . . . She's dead, Goyda. . . . What do you think of that?

GOYDA looks at KIOSK, speechless. ROSSINI nods to JANICE. They leave in separate directions.

The lights tighten on GOYDA and KIOSK.

GOYDA:
> I . . . didn't know. Nobody told me.

KIOSK: *speaking over the noise of the crowd offstage who are chanting, "Goyda, Goyda"* First my wife . . . then her. . . . I lose them both. . . . You know what that means, Goyda?

GOYDA inhales sharply, as if sobbing.

GOYDA:
Yes . . . yes . . . yes . . .

He is shouting now.

Yes!

KIOSK:
In thirty years . . . I never once took a holiday. . . . I only went to grade eight in school. . . . It's been . . . such a job . . .

He speaks with effort, continuing almost in a howl.

. . . just holding up my goddamned head among men!

The lights go out slowly on them as DOLAN sings.

DOLAN: *singing*
In our town
The roses fade
And one by one
The stones are laid
To trim the grass
Around the grave
At seven hours to sundown . . .
In our town
Seven hours to sundown.

There is a short music interlude, then abrupt silence and a blackout.

Appendix

SEVEN HOURS TO SUNDOWN

Words & Music by George Ryga

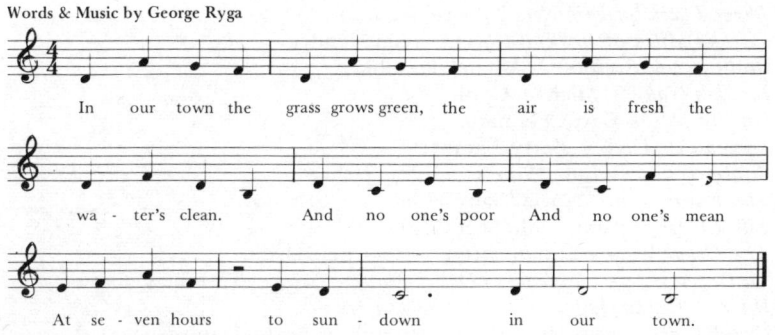

In our town the grass grows green, the air is fresh the wa-ter's clean. And no one's poor And no one's mean At se-ven hours to sun-down in our town.

TALONBOOKS — PLAYS IN PRINT 1977

Colours in the Dark — James Reaney
The Ecstasy of Rita Joe — George Ryga
Captives of the Faceless Drummer — George Ryga
Crabdance — Beverley Simons
Listen to the Wind — James Reaney
Ashes for Easter & Other Monodramas — David Watmough
Esker Mike & His Wife, Agiluk — Herschel Hardin
Sunrise on Sarah — George Ryga
Walsh — Sharon Pollock
Apple Butter & Other Plays for Children — James Reaney
The Factory Lab Anthology — Connie Brissenden, ed.
The Trial of Jean-Baptiste M. — Robert Gurik
Battering Ram — David Freeman
Hosanna — Michel Tremblay
Les Belles Soeurs — Michel Tremblay
API 2967 — Robert Gurik
You're Gonna Be Alright Jamie Boy — David Freeman
Bethune — Rod Langley
Preparing — Beverley Simons
Forever Yours Marie-Lou — Michel Tremblay
En Pièces Détachées — Michel Tremblay
Lulu Street — Ann Henry
Three Plays by Eric Nicol — Eric Nicol
Fifteen Miles of Broken Glass — Tom Hendry
Bonjour, là, Bonjour — Michel Tremblay
Jacob's Wake — Michael Cook
On the Job — David Fennario
Sqrieux-de-Dieu — Betty Lambert
Some Angry Summer Songs — John Herbert
The Execution — Marie-Claire Blais
Tiln & Other Plays — Michael Cook
The Great Wave of Civilization — Herschel Hardin
La Duchesse de Langeais & Other Plays — Michel Tremblay
Have — Julius Hay
Cruel Tears — Ken Mitchell and Humphrey & the Dumptrucks
Nothing to Lose — David Fennario
Can You See Me Yet? — Timothy Findley
Ploughmen of the Glacier — George Ryga
Les Canadiens — Rick Salutin
Seven Hours to Sundown — George Ryga
Two Plays — George Woodcock